Othniel Hermes (Ed.)

Limba–Mel Languages

Othniel Hermes (Ed.)

Limba–Mel Languages

Niger-Congo languages, Guinea-Bissau, Sierra Leone

Bellum Publishing

Cover image: www.ingimage.com
Concerning the licence of the cover image please contact ingimage.

Publisher:
Bellum Publishing is a trademark of
International Book Market Service Ltd., 17 Rue Meldrum, Beau Bassin, 1713-01 Mauritius
Email: info@bookmarketservice.com
Website: www.bookmarketservice.com

Published in 2011

Printed in: U.S.A., U.K., Germany. This book was not produced in Mauritius.

ISBN: 978-613-7-09990-2

Contents

Articles

References

Mel languages

Mel	
Southern (West) Atlantic	
Geographic distribution:	Guinea-Bissau through Liberia
Linguistic classification:	Niger–Congo • Atlantic–Congo • **Mel**
Subdivisions:	—

The **Mel languages** are a branch of Niger–Congo languages spoken in Guinea-Bissau, Guinea, Sierra Leone, and Liberia. The most populous is Temne, with about two million speakers; Kissi is next, with half a million.

Mel has traditionally been classified as a southern branch of West Atlantic. However, that is a geographic rather than genealogical group.

References

- Guillaume Serere & Florian Lionnet 2010. "'Isolates' in 'Atlantic'" [1]. *Language Isolates in Africa* workshop, Lyon, Dec. 4

References

[1] http://25images.ish-lyon.cnrs.fr/player/player.php?id=72&id_sequence=431

Mel languages

Mel	
Southern (West) Atlantic	
Geographic distribution:	Guinea-Bissau through Liberia
Linguistic classification:	Niger–Congo • Atlantic–Congo • **Mel**
Subdivisions:	—

The **Mel languages** are a branch of Niger–Congo languages spoken in Guinea-Bissau, Guinea, Sierra Leone, and Liberia. The most populous is Temne, with about two million speakers; Kissi is next, with half a million.

Mel has traditionally been classified as a southern branch of West Atlantic. However, that is a geographic rather than genealogical group.

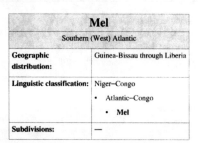

```
                       Temne
               Temne
                       Baga languages

Mel
                               Sua (Mansoanka)

                               Bullom languages
               Bullom–Kissi
                               Kissi
```

References

• Guillaume Serere & Florian Lionnet 2010. "'Isolates' in 'Atlantic'" [1]. *Language Isolates in Africa* workshop, Lyon, Dec. 4

Niger–Congo languages

Niger–Congo	
Niger–Kordofanian (obsolete)	
Geographic distribution:	Sub-Saharan Africa
Linguistic classification:	one of the world's primary language families
Subdivisions:	Dogon
	Ijoid
	? Mande
	Katla–Rashad (Kordofanian)
	Atlantic–Congo (noun classes)
ISO 639-2 and 639-5:	nic

Map showing the distribution of Niger–Congo languages (yellow). The area is divided into B (Bantu) and A (rest) to show the extent of the Bantu subfamily.

The **Niger–Congo languages** constitute one of the world's major language families, and Africa's largest in terms of geographical area, number of speakers, and number of distinct languages. They may constitute the world's largest language family in terms of distinct languages, although this question is complicated by ambiguity about what constitutes a distinct language. Most of the most widely spoken indigenous languages of Subsaharan Africa belong to this group. A common property of many Niger–Congo languages is the use of a noun class system. The most widely spoken Niger–Congo languages by number of native speakers are Yoruba, Igbo, Fula and Shona and Zulu. The most widely spoken by total number of speakers is Swahili.

Classification history

Early classifications

Niger–Congo as it is known today was only gradually recognized as a unity. In early classifications of African languages, one of the principal criteria used to distinguish different groupings was the languages' use of prefixes to classify nouns, or the lack thereof. A major advance came with the work of Koelle, who in his 1854 *Polyglotta Africana* attempted a careful classification, the groupings of which in quite a number of cases correspond to modern groupings. An early sketch of the extent of Niger–Congo as one language family can be found in Koelle's observation, echoed in Bleek (1856), that the Atlantic languages used prefixes just like many Southern African languages. Subsequent work of Bleek, and some decades later the comparative work of Meinhof, solidly established Bantu as a linguistic unit.

In many cases, wider classifications employed a blend of typological and racial criteria. Thus, Friedrich Müller, in his ambitious classification (1876–88), separated the 'Negro' and Bantu languages. Likewise, the Africanist Lepsius considered Bantu to be of African origin, and many 'Mixed Negro languages' as products of an encounter between Bantu and intruding Asiatic languages.

In this period a relation between Bantu and languages with Bantu-like (but less complete) noun class systems began to emerge. Some authors saw the latter as languages which had not yet completely evolved to full Bantu status, whereas others regarded them as languages which had partly lost original features still found in Bantu. The Bantuist Meinhof made a major distinction between Bantu and a 'Semi-Bantu' group which according to him was originally of the unrelated Sudanic stock.

Westermann, Greenberg and beyond

Westermann, a pupil of Meinhof, set out to establish the internal classification of the then Sudanic languages. In a 1911 work he established a basic division between 'East' and 'West'. A historical reconstruction of West Sudanic was published in 1927, and in his 1935 'Charakter und Einteilung der Sudansprachen' he conclusively established the relationship between Bantu and West Sudanic.

Joseph Greenberg took Westermann's work as a starting-point for his own classification. In a series of articles published between 1949 and 1954, he argued that Westermann's 'West Sudanic' and Bantu formed a single genetic family, which he named Niger–Congo; that Bantu constituted a subgroup of the Benue–Congo branch; that Adamawa–Eastern, previously not considered to be related, was another member of this family; and that Fula belonged to the West Atlantic languages. Just before these articles were collected in final book form (*The Languages of Africa*) in 1963, he amended his classification by adding Kordofanian as a branch co-ordinate with Niger–Congo as a whole; consequently, he renamed the family *Congo–Kordofanian*, later *Niger–Kordofanian*. Greenberg's work, though initially greeted with scepticism, became the prevailing view among scholars.

Westermann's 1911 *Die Sudansprachen. Eine sprachvergleichende Studie* laid much of the basis for the understanding of Niger–Congo.

Bennet and Sterk (1977) presented an internal reclassification based on lexicostatistics that laid the foundation for the regrouping in Bendor-Samuel (1989). Kordofanian was thought to be one of several primary branches rather than being coordinate to the phylum as a whole, prompting re-introduction of the term *Niger–Congo*, which is in current use among linguists. Many classifications continue to place Kordofanian as the most distant branch, but mainly due to negative evidence (fewer lexical correspondences), rather than positive evidence that the other languages form a valid genealogical group. Likewise, Mande is often assumed to be the second-most distant branch based on its lack of the noun-class system prototypical of the Niger–Congo family. Other branches lacking any trace of the noun-class system are Dogon and Ijaw, whereas the Talodi branch of Kordofanian does have cognate noun classes, suggesting that Kordofanian is also not a unitary group.

Niger–Congo and Nilo-Saharan

Over the years, several linguists have suggested a link between Niger–Congo and Nilo-Saharan, probably starting with Westermann's comparative work on the 'Sudanic' family in which 'Eastern Sudanic' (now classified as Nilo-Saharan) and 'Western Sudanic' (now classified as Niger–Congo) were united. Gregersen (1972) proposed that Niger–Congo and Nilo-Saharan be united into a larger phylum which he termed *Kongo–Saharan*. His evidence was mainly based on the uncertainty in the classification of Songhay, morphological resemblances, and lexical similarities. A more recent proponent was Roger Blench (1995), who puts forward phonological, morphological and lexical evidence for uniting Niger–Congo and Nilo-Saharan in a *Niger–Saharan* phylum, with special affinity between Niger–Congo and Central Sudanic. However, fifteen years later his views had changed, with Blench (2011) proposing instead that the noun-classifier system of Central Sudanic, commonly reflected in a tripartite general–singulative–plurative number system, triggered the development or elaboration of the noun-class system of the Atlantic–Congo languages, with tripartite number marking surviving in the Plateau and Gur languages of Niger–Congo, and the lexical similarities being due to loans.

Common features

Phonology

Niger–Congo languages have a clear preference for open syllables of the type CV (Consonant Vowel). The typical word structure of Proto-Niger–Congo is thought to have been CVCV, a structure still attested in, for example, Bantu, Mande and Ijoid – in many other branches this structure has been reduced through phonological change. Verbs are composed of a root followed by one or more extensional suffixes. Nouns consist of a root originally preceded by a noun class prefix of (C)V- shape which is often eroded by phonological change.

Consonant and vowel systems

Reconstructions of the consonant system of several branches of Niger–Congo (Stewart for proto-Volta–Congo, Mukarovsky for his proto-West-Nigritic, roughly corresponding to Atlantic–Congo) have posited independently a regular phonological contrast between two classes of consonants. Pending more clarity as to the precise nature of this contrast it is commonly characterized as a contrast between 'fortis' and 'lenis' consonants. Five places of articulation are postulated for the consonant inventory of proto-Niger–Congo: labial, alveolar, palatal, velar, and labial-velar.

Many Niger–Congo languages show vowel harmony based on the feature [ATR] (advanced tongue root). In this type of vowel harmony, the position of the root of the tongue is the phonetic basis for the distinction between two harmonizing sets of vowels. In its fullest form, this type involves two classes, each of five vowels: [+ATR] /i, e, ə, o, u/ and [-ATR] /ɪ, ɛ, a, ɔ, ʊ/. Vowel inventories of this type are still found in some branches of Niger–Congo, for example in the Ghana Togo Mountain languages.[1] To date, many languages show reductions from this fuller system. The fact that ten vowels have been reconstructed for proto-Atlantic, proto-Ijoid and possibly proto-Volta–Congo leads Williamson (1989:23) to the hypothesis that the original vowel inventory of Niger–Congo was a full ten-vowel system. On the other hand, Stewart in recent comparative work reconstructs a seven vowel system for his proto-Potou-Akanic-Bantu.[2]

Nasality

Several scholars have documented a contrast between oral and nasal vowels in Niger–Congo.[3] In his reconstruction of proto-Volta–Congo, Steward (1976) postulates that nasal consonants have originated under the influence of nasal vowels; this hypothesis is supported by the fact that there are several Niger–Congo languages that have been analysed as lacking nasal consonants altogether. Languages like this have nasal vowels accompanied with complementary distribution between oral and nasal consonants before oral and nasal vowels. Subsequent loss of the nasal/oral contrast in vowels may result in nasal consonants becoming part of the phoneme inventory. In all cases reported to date, the bilabial /m/ is the first nasal consonant to be phonologized. Niger–Congo thus invalidates two common assumptions about nasals[4] : that all languages have at least one primary nasal consonant, and that if a language has only one primary nasal consonant it is /n/.

Niger–Congo languages commonly show fewer nasalized than oral vowels. Kasem, a language with a ten-vowel system employing ATR vowel harmony, has seven nasalized vowels. Similarly, Yoruba has seven oral vowels and only five nasal ones. However, the recently discovered language of Zialo has nasal equivalent for each of its seven vowels.

Tone

The large majority of present-day Niger–Congo languages are tonal. A typical Niger–Congo tone system involves two or three contrastive level tones. Four level systems are less widespread, and five level systems are rare. Only a few Niger–Congo languages are non-tonal; Swahili is perhaps the best known, but within the Atlantic branch some others are found. Proto-Niger–Congo is thought to have been a tone language with two contrastive levels. Synchronic and comparative-historical studies of tone systems show that such a basic system can easily develop more tonal contrasts under the influence of depressor consonants or through the introduction of a downstep. Languages which have more tonal levels tend to use tone more for lexical and less for grammatical contrasts.

Contrastive levels of tone in some Niger–Congo languages

H, L	Dyula–Bambara, Maninka, Temne, Dogon, Dagbani, Gbaya, Efik, Lingala
H, M, L	Yakuba, Nafaanra, Kasem, Banda, Yoruba, Jukun, Dangme, Yukuben, Akan, Anyi, Ewe, Igbo
T, H, M, L	Gban, Wobe, Munzombo, Igede, Mambila, Fon
T, H, M, L, B	Ashuku (Benue–Congo), Dan-Santa (Mande)
PA/S	Mandinka (Senegambia), Fula, Wolof, Kimwani
none	Swahili

Abbreviations used: T top, H high, M mid, L low, B bottom, PA/S pitch-accent or stress
Adapted from Williamson 1989:27

Morphosyntax

Noun classification

Niger–Congo languages are known for their system of noun classification, traces of which can be found in every branch of the family but Mande, Ijoid, Dogon, and the Katla and Rashad branches of Kordofanian. These noun-classification systems are somewhat analogous to grammatical gender in other languages, but there are often a fairly large number of classes (often 10 or more), and the classes may be male human/female human/animate/inanimate, or even completely gender-unrelated categories such as places, plants, abstracts, and groups of objects. For example, in Bantu, the Swahili language is called *Kiswahili*, while the Swahili people are *Waswahili*. Likewise, in Ubangian, the Zande language is called *Pazande*, while the Zande people are called *Azande*.

In the Bantu languages, where noun classification is particularly elaborate, it typically appears as prefixes, with verbs and adjectives marked according to the class of the noun they refer to. For example, in Swahili, *watu wazuri wataenda* is 'good *(zuri)* people *(tu)* will go *(ta-enda)*'.

Verbal extensions

The same Atlantic–Congo languages which have noun classes also have a set of verb applicatives and other verbal extensions, such as the reciprocal suffix *-na* (Swahili *penda* 'to love', *pendana* 'to love each other'; also applicative *pendea* 'to love for' and causative *pendeza* 'to please').

Word order

A subject–verb–object word order is quite widespread among today's Niger–Congo languages, but SOV is found in branches as divergent as Mande, Ijoid and Dogon. As a result, there has been quite some debate as to the basic word order of Niger–Congo.

Whereas Claudi (1993) argues for SVO on the basis of existing SVO>SOV grammaticalization paths (SOV>SVO is never found), Gensler (1997) points out that the notion of 'basic word order' is problematic as it excludes structures with, for example, auxiliaries. However, the structure SC-OC-VbStem (Subject concord, Object concord, Verb stem) found in the "verbal complex" of the SVO Bantu languages suggests an earlier SOV pattern (where the subject and object were at least represented by pronouns).

Noun phrases in most Niger–Congo languages are characteristically *noun-initial*, with adjectives, numerals, demonstratives and genitives all coming after the noun. The major exceptions are found in the western[5] areas where verb-final word order predominates and genitives precede nouns, though other modifiers still come afterwards. Degree words almost always follow adjectives, and except in verb-final languages adpositions are prepositional.

The verb-final languages of the Mende region have two quite unusual word order characteristics. Although verbs follow their direct objects, oblique adpositional phrases (like "in the house", "with timber") typically come after the verb,[5] creating a **SOVX** word order. Also noteworthy in these languages is the prevalence of internally-headed and correlative relative clauses, in both of which the head occurs *inside* the relative clause rather than the main clause.

Major clades

The traditional branches and major languages of the Niger–Congo family are,[6]

- Kordofanian languages: spoken in southern central Sudan, around the Nuba Mountains (not a single family)
- ? Mande: spoken in West Africa; includes Bambara, the main language spoken in Mali, as well as Soninke, a language spoken mainly in Mali but also in Senegal and Mauritania. The evidence linking Mande to Niger–Congo is thin. Blench regards it as an early branch that diverged before the morphology characteristic of most of Niger–Congo developed, which Dimmendaal (2008) argues that for now it is best considered an independent family.
- Ijoid in Nigeria, including Ijo and Defaka.
- ? Dogon, spoken in Mali. The evidence linking Dogon to Niger–Congo is weak.
- Atlantic: includes Wolof, spoken in Senegal, and Fula, a language spoken across the Sahel. The validity of Atlantic as a genetic grouping is controversial.
- Kru: spoken in West Africa, include Bété, Nyabwa, and Dida.
- Senufo: spoken in Côte d'Ivoire and Mali, with a geographical outlier in Ghana, and including Senari and Supyire.
- Savannahs: Including Gur languages such as More in Burkina Faso, and the Adamawa languages.
- ? Ubangi languages: such as Sango in the Central African Republic. Olson (2006:165-167) demonstrated that the evidence linking Ubangian to Niger–Congo is weak, and Dimmendal (2008) went so far as to exclude Ubangian from Niger–Congo.[7]
- Kwa: includes Akan, spoken in Ghana.
- Volta–Niger (= West Benue–Congo), including among others:
  - The Gbe languages, spoken in Ghana, Togo, Benin, and Nigeria, of which Ewe is best known.
  - The Yoruba and Igbo languages, spoken in Nigeria.
- (East) Benue–Congo, including:

- The very large Bantu family, with Swahili, Fang, Kongo, Zulu, and many other languages of central and southern Africa.

Some linguists consider the twenty or so Kordofanian languages to form part of the Niger–Congo family, while others consider them and Niger–Congo to form two separate branches of a *Niger–Kordofanian* language family, and yet others do not accept Kordofanian as a single group. Senufo has been placed traditionally within Gur, but is now usually considered an early off-shoot from Atlantic–Congo.

The Laal, Mpre, and Jalaa languages are often linked with Niger–Congo, but have yet to be conclusively classified.

Localization of the Niger–Congo languages

Notes

[1] See for example Logba: linguistic features for a Ghana Togo Mountain language with a nine vowel system employing ATR vowel harmony.

[2] Stewart (1976) for proto-Volta–Congo (see also Casali 1995), Doneux (1975) for proto-Atlantic, Williamson (n.d.) for proto-Ijoid, and Stewart (2002:208) for Proto-Potou-Akanic-Bantu.

[3] le Saout (1973) for an early overview, Stewart (1976) for a diachronic, Volta–Congo wide analysis, Capo (1981) for a synchronic analysis of nasality in Gbe (see Gbe languages: nasality), and Bole-Richard (1984, 1985) as cited in Williamson (1989) for similar reports on several Mande, Gur, Kru, Kwa, and Ubangi languages.)

[4] As noted by Williamson (1989:24). The assumptions are from Ferguson's (1963) 'Assumptions about nasals' in Greenberg (ed.) *Universals of Language*, pp 50–60 as cited in Williamson art.cit.

[5] Haspelmath, Martin; Dryer, Matthew S.; Gil, David and Comrie, Bernard (eds.) *The World Atlas of Language Structures*; pp 346–385. Oxford: Oxford University Press, 2005. ISBN 0-19-925591-1

[6] Williamson & Blench (2000)

[7] Dimmendaal (2008) states that Ubangian "probably constitutes an independent language family that cannot or can no longer be shown to be related to Niger–Congo (or any other family)." (Gerrit Dimmendaal, "Language Ecology and Linguistic Diversity on the African Continent", *Language and Linguistics Compass* 2/5:841.

Further reading

- Vic Webb (2001) *African Voices: An Introduction to the Languages and Linguistics of Africa*
- Bendor-Samuel, John & Rhonda L. Hartell (eds.) (1989) *The Niger–Congo Languages – A classification and description of Africa's largest language family*. Lanham, Maryland: University Press of America.
- Bennett, Patrick R. & Sterk, Jan P. (1977) 'South Central Niger–Congo: A reclassification'. *Studies in African Linguistics*, 8, 241–273.
- Blench, Roger (1995) 'Is Niger–Congo simply a branch of Nilo-Saharan?' In *Proceedings: Fifth Nilo-Saharan Linguistics Colloquium, Nice, 1992*, ed. R. Nicolai and F. Rottland, 83-130. Köln: Rüdiger Köppe.
- —— (2011) "Can Sino-Tibetan and Austroasiatic help us understand the evolution of Niger-Congo noun classes?", (http://media.leidenuniv.nl/legacy/blench-call-leiden-2011.pdf) CALL 41, Leiden
- Capo, Hounkpati B.C. (1981) 'Nasality in Gbe: A Synchronic Interpretation' *Studies in African Linguistics*, 12, 1, 1-43.
- Casali, Roderic F. (1995) 'On the Reduction of Vowel Systems in Volta–Congo', *African Languages and Cultures*, 8, 2, December, 109–121.
- Dimmendaal, Gerrit (2008) 'Language Ecology and Linguistic Diversity on the African Continent', *Language and Linguistics Compass* 2/5:841.
- Greenberg, Joseph H. (1963) *The Languages of Africa*. Indiana University Press.
- Gregersen, Edgar A. (1972) 'Kongo-Saharan'. *Journal of African Linguistics*, 4, 46-56.
- Olson, Kenneth S. (2006) 'On Niger–Congo classification'. In *The Bill question*, ed. H. Aronson, D. Dyer, V. Friedman, D. Hristova and J. Sadock, 153–190. Bloomington, IN: Slavica.
- Saout, J. le (1973) 'Languages sans consonnes nasales', *Annales de l Université d'Abidjan*, H, 6, 1, 179-205.
- Stewart, John M. (1976) *Towards Volta–Congo reconstruction: a comparative study of some languages of Black-Africa*. (Inaugural speech, Leiden University) Leiden: Universitaire Pers Leiden.
- Stewart, John M. (2002) 'The potential of Proto-Potou-Akanic-Bantu as a pilot Proto-Niger–Congo, and the reconstructions updated', in *Journal of African Languages and Linguistics*, 23, 197-224.
- Williamson, Kay (1989) 'Niger–Congo overview', in Bendor-Samuel & Hartell (eds.) *The Niger–Congo Languages*, 3-45.
- Williamson, Kay & Blench, Roger (2000) 'Niger–Congo', in Heine, Bernd and Nurse, Derek (eds) *African Languages – An Introduction*. Cambridge: Cambridge University Press, pp. 11–42.

External links

- An Evaluation of Niger–Congo Classification (http://www.sil.org/silewp/2004/silewp2004-005.pdf), Kenneth Olson
- Ethnologue: Niger–Congo Family Tree (http://www.ethnologue.com/show_family.asp?subid=68-16)
- The LINGUIST List MultiTree Project: Niger–Congo Family Trees (http://multitree.linguistlist.org/codes/ncon)
- International Niger–Congo Reconstruction Project (http://www.nigercongo.com)

Guinea-Bissau

Republic of Guinea-Bissau *República da Guiné-Bissau*	
Motto: Portuguese: *"Unidade, Luta, Progresso"* *"Unity, Struggle, Progress"*	
Anthem: Portuguese: *"Esta é a Nossa Pátria Bem Amada"* *"This is Our Well-Beloved Motherland"*	
Capital (and largest city)	Bissau 11°52′N 15°36′W
Official language(s)	Portuguese
Recognised regional languages	Crioulo
Demonym	Bissau-Guinean(s)[1]
Government	Semi-presidential republic
- President	Malam Bacai Sanhá
- Prime Minister	Carlos Gomes
Independence	from Portugal
- Declared	September 24, 1973
- Recognized	September 10, 1974
Area	
- Total	36,125 km^2 (136th) 13,948 sq mi
- Water (%)	22.4
Population	
- 2010 estimate	1,647,000[2] (148th)
- 2002 census	1,345,479

-	Density	44.1/km² (154th) 115.5/sq mi
GDP (PPP)		2010 estimate
-	Total	$1.784 billion[3]
-	Per capita	$1,084[3]
GDP (nominal)		2010 estimate
-	Total	$837 million[3]
-	Per capita	$508[3]
Gini (1993)		47 (high)
HDI (2010)		0.289 (low) (164th)
Currency		West African CFA franc (XOF)
Time zone		GMT (UTC+0)
Drives on the		left
Internet TLD		.gw
Calling code		245

The **Republic of Guinea-Bissau** /'gɪnibɪ'saʊ/ (Portuguese: *República da Guiné-Bissau*, pronounced [ʁe'publikɐ dɐ gi'nɛ bi'saw]) is a country in West Africa. It is bordered by Senegal to the north, and Guinea to the south and east, with the Atlantic Ocean to its west.

It covers 36,125 km² (nearly 14,000 sq mi) with an estimated population of 1,600,000.

Guinea-Bissau was once part of the kingdom of Gabu, as well as part of the Mali Empire. Parts of this kingdom persisted until the 18th century, while a few others were part of the Portuguese Empire since the 16th century. It then became the Portuguese colony of Portuguese Guinea in the 19th century. Upon independence, declared in 1973 and recognised in 1974, the name of its capital, Bissau, was added to the country's name to prevent confusion with the Republic of Guinea.

Only 14% of the population speaks the official language, Portuguese. A plurality of the population (44%) speaks Kriol, a Portuguese-based creole language, and the remainder speak native African languages. The main religions are African traditional religions and Islam, and there is a Christian (mostly Catholic) minority.

Guinea-Bissau is a member of the African Union, Economic Community of West African States, Organisation of Islamic Cooperation, the Latin Union, Community of Portuguese Language Countries, La Francophonie and the South Atlantic Peace and Cooperation Zone.

The country's per-capita gross domestic product is one of the lowest in the world.

History

Guinea-Bissau was once part of the kingdom of Gabu, part of the Mali Empire; parts of this kingdom persisted until the 18th century, while others were part of the Portuguese Empire. Portuguese Guinea was known also, from its main economic activity, as the Slave Coast.

Early reports of Europeans reaching this area include those of the Venetian Alvise Cadamosto's voyage of 1455, the 1479-1480 voyage by Flemish-French trader Eustache de la Fosse, and Diogo Cão who in the 1480s reached the Congo River and the lands of Bakongo, setting up thus the foundations of modern Angola, some 1200 km down the African coast from Guinea-Bissau.

Although the rivers and coast of this area were among the first places colonized by the Portuguese, since the 16th century, the interior was not explored until the 19th century. The local African rulers in Guinea, some of whom prospered greatly from the slave trade, had no interest in allowing the Europeans any further inland than the fortified coastal settlements where the trading took place. African communities that fought back against slave traders had even greater incentives to distrust European adventurers and would-be settlers. The Portuguese presence in Guinea was therefore largely limited to the port of Bissau and Cacheu, although isolated European farmer-settlers established farms along Bissau's inland rivers.

Portuguese-held (green), disputed (yellow) and rebel-held areas (red) in Portuguese-Guinea and other colonies 1970

For a brief period in the 1790s the British attempted to establish a rival foothold on an offshore island, at Bolama. But by the 19th century the Portuguese were sufficiently secure in Bissau to regard the neighbouring coastline as their own special territory, also up north in part of present South Senegal.

An armed rebellion beginning in 1956 by the African Party for the Independence of Guinea and Cape Verde (PAIGC) under the leadership of Amílcar Cabral gradually consolidated its hold on then Portuguese Guinea. Unlike guerrilla movements in other Portuguese colonies, the PAIGC rapidly extended its military control over large portions of the territory, aided by the jungle-like terrain, its easily reached borderlines with neighbouring allies and large quantities of arms from Cuba, China, the Soviet Union, and left-leaning African countries.

Cuba also agreed to supply artillery experts, doctors and technicians.[4] The PAIGC even managed to acquire a significant anti-aircraft capability in order to defend itself against aerial attack. By 1973, the PAIGC was in control of many parts of Guinea. Independence was unilaterally declared on September 24, 1973. Recognition became universal following the April 25, 1974 socialist-inspired military coup in Portugal which overthrew Lisbon's Estado Novo regime.

Independence

Luís Cabral was appointed the first President of Guinea-Bissau. Following independence local black soldiers that fought along with the Portuguese Army against the PAIGC guerrillas were slaughtered by the thousands. Some managed to escape and settled in Portugal or other African nations, one of the massacres occurred in the town of Bissorã. In 1980 the PAIGC admitted in its newspaper "Nó Pintcha" (dated November 29, 1980) that many were executed and buried in unmarked collective graves in the woods of Cumerá, Portogole and Mansabá.

The country was controlled by a revolutionary council until 1984. The first multi-party elections were held in 1994, but an army uprising in 1998 led to the president's ousting and the Guinea-Bissau Civil War. Elections were held again in 2000 and Kumba Ialá was elected president.

In September 2003, a coup took place in which the military arrested Ialá on the charge of being "unable to solve the problems." After being delayed several times, legislative elections were held in March 2004 . A mutiny of military factions in October 2004 resulted in the death of the head of the armed forces, and caused widespread unrest.

The Vieira years

Map of Guinea Bissau

In June 2005, presidential elections were held for the first time since the coup that deposed Ialá. Ialá returned as the candidate for the PRS, claiming to be the legitimate president of the country, but the election was won by former president João Bernardo Vieira, deposed in the 1999 coup. Vieira beat Malam Bacai Sanhá in a runoff election, but Sanhá initially refused to concede, claiming that tampering occurred in two constituencies including the capital, Bissau.

Despite reports that there had been an influx of arms in the weeks leading up to the election and reports of some "disturbances during campaigning"—including attacks on government offices by unidentified gunmen—foreign election monitors labelled the election as "calm and organized".[5] PAIGC won a strong parliamentary majority, with 67 of 100 seats, in the parliamentary election held in November 2008.

In November 2008, President Vieira's official residence was attacked by members of the armed forces, killing a guard but leaving the president unharmed.[6] On March 2, 2009, however, Vieira was assassinated by what preliminary reports indicated to be a group of soldiers avenging the death of the head of joint chiefs of staff, General Batista Tagme Na Wai. Tagme died in an explosion on Sunday, March 1, 2009 in an assassination. Military leaders in the country have pledged to respect the constitutional order of succession. National Assembly Speaker Raimundo Pereira was appointed as an interim president until a nationwide election on June 28, 2009,[7] which was won by Malam Bacai Sanhá.

2010 Guinea-Bissau military unrest

Military unrest occurred in Guinea-Bissau on 1 April 2010. Prime Minister Carlos Gomes Junior was placed under house arrest by soldiers, who also detained Army Chief of Staff Zamora Induta. Supporters of Gomes and his party, PAIGC, reacted to the move by demonstrating in the capital, Bissau; Antonio Indjai, the Deputy Chief of Staff, then warned that he would have Gomes killed if the protests continued.[8]

The EU ended its mission to reform the country's security forces 4 August 2010, a risk that may further embolden powerful generals and drug traffickers in the army and elsewhere. The EU mission's spokesman in Guinea-Bissau, Miguel Souza, said the EU had to suspend its programme when the mastermind of the mutiny, Gen Antonio Indjai, became army chief of staff. "The EU mission thinks this is a breach in the constitutional order. We can't work with him".[9]

Angolan Military Mission in Guinea-Bissau (MISSANG)

On 10 September 2010, Angola and Guinea Bissau signed a protocol in which Angola will assist the Guinean Armed and Police Forces during two years. Approximately 200 Angolan Armed Forces personnel will support the Angolan Military Mission in Guinea-Bissau (MISSANG) which was formally launched on 21 March 2011.[10] Officials in Angola said the goal was to help Guinea-Bissau end the military coups and drug trafficking that have plagued the tiny west African state for decades.[11]

Drug Trade

The multitude of small offshore islands and a military able to sidestep government with impunity has made it a favourite trans-shipment point for drugs to Europe. Plane drops are made on or near the islands, and speedboats pick up bales to go direct to Europe or onshore.[12] UN chief Ban Ki-moon has called for sanctions against those involved in Guinea-Bissau's drugs trade.[13] Air force head Ibraima Papa Camara and former navy chief Jose Americo Bubo Na Tchuto have been named "drug kingpins".[14]

Politics

Guinea-Bissau is a republic. In the past, the government had been highly centralized, and multiparty governance has been in effect since mid-1991. The president is the head of state and the prime minister is the head of government. At the legislative level, there is a unicameral "Assembleia Nacional Popular" (National People's Assembly) made up of 100 members. They are popularly elected from multi-member constituencies to serve a four-year term. At the judicial level, there is a "Tribunal Supremo da Justiça" (Supreme Court) which consists of nine justices appointed by the president, they serve at the pleasure of the president.

Ministry of Justice, Bissau

The current President of Guinea-Bissau is Rachide Sambu-balde Malam Bacai Sanhá of the PAIGC (Partido da Africa Independencia da Guine-Bissau e Cape Verde) one of two major political parties in Guinea-Bissau along with the PRS (Partido Renovacao Social) and alongside over twenty smaller parties. In the 2009 election to replace the assassinated Vieira, Sanhá was the presidential candidate of the PAIGC while Kumba Iala, was the presidential candidate of the PRS.

Until March 2009 João Bernardo "Nino" Vieira was President of Guinea-Bissau. Elected in 2005 as an independent candidate, being declared winner of the second round by the CNE (Comite Nacional da Eleicoes). Vieira returned to power in 2005 after winning the presidential election only six years after being ousted from office during a civil war. Previously, he held power for 19 years after taking power in 1980 in a bloodless coup. In that action, he toppled the government of Luís Cabral. He was killed on March 2, 2009, possibly by soldiers in retaliation for the killing of the head of the joint chiefs of staff, General Batista Tagme Na Waie.[15] This did not trigger additional violence, but there were signs of turmoil in the country, according to the advocacy group swisspeace.[16]

Regions and sectors

Guinea-Bissau is divided into 8 regions (*regiões*) and one autonomous sector (*sector autónomo*). These in turn are subdivided into thirty-seven sectors. The regions are:

- Bafatá
- Biombo
- Bissau*
- Bolama
- Cacheu
- Gabu
- Oio
- Quinara
- Tombali

* autonomous sector

Geography

Guinea-Bissau lies mostly between latitudes 11° and 13°N (a small area is south of 11°), and longitudes 13° and 17°W.

At 36125 square kilometres (13948 sq mi), the country is larger in size than Taiwan, Belgium, or the U.S. state of Maryland. This small, tropical country lies at a low altitude; its highest point is 300 metres (984 ft). The interior is savanna, and the coastline is plain with swamps of Guinean mangroves. Its monsoon-like rainy season alternates with periods of hot, dry harmattan winds blowing from the Sahara. The Bijagos Archipelago extends out to sea.

Typical scenery in Guinea-Bissau

Major cities

Main cities in Guinea-Bissau include:

Satellite image of Guinea-Bissau (2003)

Rank	City	Population		Region
		1979 Census	2005 estimate	
1	Bissau	109,214	388,028	Bissau
2	Bafatá	13,429	22,521	Bafatá
3	Gabú	7,803	14,430	Gabú
4	Bissorã	N/A	12,688	Oio
5	Bolama	9,100	10,769	Bolama
6	Cacheu	7,600	10,490	Cacheu
7	Bubaque	8,400	9,941	Bolama
8	Catió	5,170	9,898	Tombali
9	Mansôa	5,390	7,821	Oio
10	Buba	N/A	7,779	Quinara
11	Quebo	N/A	7,072	Quinara
12	Canchungo	4,965	6,853	Cacheu
13	Farim	4,468	6,792	Oio
14	Quinhámel	N/A	3,128	Biombo
15	Fulacunda	N/A	1,327	Quinara

Climate

Quelle: Geoklima 2.1

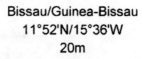

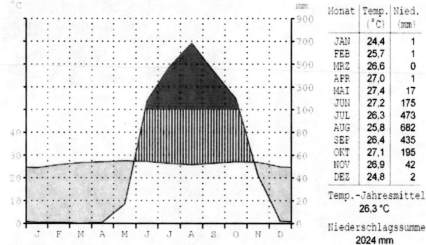

Bissau/Guinea-Bissau
11°52'N/15°36'W
20m

Monat	Temp. (°C)	Nied. (mm)
JAN	24,4	1
FEB	25,7	1
MRZ	26,6	0
APR	27,0	1
MAI	27,4	17
JUN	27,2	175
JUL	26,3	473
AUG	25,8	682
SEP	26,4	435
OKT	27,1	195
NOV	26,9	42
DEZ	24,8	2

Temp.-Jahresmittel
26,3 °C

Niederschlagssumme
2024 mm

Guinea-Bissau is warm all year around and there is little temperature fluctuation; it averages 26.3 °C (79.3 °F). The average rainfall for Bissau is 2024 millimetres (79.7 in) although this is almost entirely accounted for during the rainy season which falls between June and September/October. From December through April, the country experiences drought.

Economy

Guinea-Bissau's GDP per capita is one of the lowest in the world. Its Human Development Index is also one of the lowest on earth. More than two-thirds of the population lives below the poverty line. The economy depends mainly on agriculture; fish, cashew nuts and ground nuts are its major exports. A long period of political instability has resulted in depressed economic activity, deteriorating social conditions, and increased macroeconomic imbalances.

Guinea-Bissau has started to show some economic advances after a pact of stability was signed by the main political parties of the country, leading to an IMF-backed structural reform program. The key challenges for the country in the period ahead would be to achieve fiscal discipline, rebuild public administration, improve the economic climate for private investment, and promote economic diversification. After becoming independent from Portugal in 1974 due to the Portuguese Colonial War and the Carnation Revolution, the exodus of the Portuguese civilian, military and political authorities brought tremendous damage to the country's economic infrastructure, social order and standard of living.

After several years of economic downturn and political instability, in 1997, Guinea-Bissau entered the CFA franc monetary system, bringing about some internal monetary stability. The civil war that took place in 1998 and 1999 and a military coup in September 2003 again disrupted economic activity, leaving a substantial part of the economic and social infrastructure in ruins and intensifying the already widespread poverty. Following the parliamentary elections in March 2004 and presidential elections in July 2005, the country is trying to recover from the long period of instability despite a still-fragile political situation.

Beginning around 2005, drug traffickers based in Latin America began to use Guinea-Bissau, along with several neighboring West African nations, as a transshipment point to Europe for cocaine. The nation was described by a United Nations official as being at risk for becoming a "narco-state".The government and the military did almost nothing to stop this business. In 2009 nearly all transports via Guinea Bissau have been stopped and translocated to Mali.[17] [18]

Bula, Guinea-Bissau

Guinea-Bissau is a member of the Organization for the Harmonization of Business Law in Africa (OHADA).[19]

Carnival in Bissau.

Demographics

Crossing the river at low tide

Religion in Guinea-Bissau[20] [21]	
religion	percent
Islam	50%
Indigenous	40%
Christianity	10%

Ethnic groups

The population of Guinea-Bissau is ethnically diverse and has many distinct languages, customs, and social structures. Guinea-Bissauans can be divided into the following ethnic groups: Fula and the Mandinka-speaking people, who comprise the largest portion of the population and are concentrated in the north and northeast; the Balanta and Papel people, who live in the southern coastal regions; and the Manjaco and Mancanha, who occupy the central and northern coastal areas. Most of the remainder are *mestiços* of mixed Portuguese and African descent, including a Cape Verdean minority.

Portuguese natives comprise a very small percentage of Guinea-Bissauans. This deficit was directly caused by the exodus of Portuguese settlers that took place after Guinea-Bissau gained independence. The country has also a tiny Chinese population, including those of mixed Portuguese and Chinese ancestry from Macau, a former Asian Portuguese colony.

Language

Only 14% of the population speaks the official language, Portuguese. 44% speak Kriol, a Portuguese-based creole language, and the remainder speaks native African languages. Most Portuguese and Mestiços speak one of the African languages and Kriol as second languages. French is also learned in schools, as the country is surrounded by French-speaking countries and is a full member of the Francophonie.

Religion

Throughout the 20th century, most Bissau-Guineans practiced some form of Animism. Recently, many have adopted Islam, which is currently practiced by 35 percent of the country's population; most of Guinea-Bissau's Muslims practice Sunni Islam. Approximately 10 percent of the country's population belong to the Christian community, and 55 percent continue to hold Indigenous beliefs. These statistics can be misleading, however, as both Islamic and Christan practices may be largely influenced and enriched by syncretism with traditional African beliefs.[20] [21]

Health

The WHO estimates that there are fewer than 5 physicians per 100,000 persons in the country,[22] down from 12 per 100,000 in 2007.[23] The prevalence of HIV-infection among the adult population is 1.8%,[24] with only 20% of infected pregnant women receiving anti retroviral coverage.[25] Malaria is an even bigger killer; 9% of the population have reported infection,[26] and it is the specific mortality cause almost three times as often as AIDS.[27] (In 2008, fewer than half of children younger than five slept under antimalaria nets or had access to antimalarial drugs).[28]

Maternal and Child Healthcare

In June 2011, the United Nations Population Fund released a report on The State of the World's Midwifery [29]. It contained new data on the midwifery workforce and policies relating to newborn and maternal mortality for 58 countries. The 2010 maternal mortality rate per 100,000 births for Guinea Bissau is 1000. This is compared with 804.3 in 2008 and 966 in 1990. The under 5 mortality rate, per 1,000 births is 195 and the neonatal mortality as a percentage of under 5's mortality is 24. The aim of this report is to highlight ways in which the Millennium Development Goals can be achieved, particularly Goal 4 – Reduce child mortality and Goal 5 – improve maternal death. In Guinea Bissau the number of midwives per 1,000 live births is 3 and 1 in 18 shows us the lifetime risk of death for pregnant women. [30]

Education

Education is compulsory from the age of 7 to 13.[31] The enrollment of boys is higher than that of girls.[31] Child labor is very common.[31] A significant minority of the population are illiterate.[32]

On the other side, Guinea-Bissau has several secondary schools (general as well as technical) and a surprising number of universities, to which an institutionally autonomous Faculty of Law as well as a Faculty of Medicine [33] have to be added.

Life expectancy at birth has climbed since 1990, but remains short: the WHO's estimate of life expectancy for a child born in 2008 was 49 years (and only 47 years for a boy).[34]

Music

The music of Guinea-Bissau is usually associated with the polyrhythmic gumbe genre, the country's primary musical export. However, civil unrest and other factors have combined over the years to keep gumbe, and other genres, out of mainstream audiences, even in generally syncretist African countries.

The calabash is the primary musical instrument of Guinea-Bissau, and is used in extremely swift and rhythmically complex dance music. Lyrics are almost always in Guinea-Bissau Creole, a Portuguese-based creole language, and are often humorous and topical, revolving around current events and controversies, especially AIDS.

The word *gumbe* is sometimes used generically, to refer to any music of the country, although it most specifically refers to a unique style that fuses about ten of the country's folk music traditions. Tina and tinga are other popular genres, while extent folk traditions include ceremonial music used in funerals, initiations and other rituals, as well as Balanta brosca and kussundé, Mandinga djambadon, and the kundere sound of the Bissagos Islands.

Film

Flora Gomes is an internationally renowned film director; his most famous film is *Nha Fala*.

See also

Additional, more specific, and related topics may be found at:

- Foreign relations of Guinea-Bissau
- Military of Guinea-Bissau
- Transport in Guinea-Bissau
- Corpo Nacional de Escutas da Guiné-Bissau
- 2010 Guinea-Bissau military unrest

References

[1] "Background Note: Guinea-Bissau" (http://www.state.gov/r/pa/ei/bgn/5454.htm). US Department of State. December, 2009. . Retrieved 7 February 2010.

[2] Department of Economic and Social Affairs Population Division (2009) (PDF). *World Population Prospects, Table A.1* (http://www.un. org/esa/population/publications/wpp2008/wpp2008_text_tables.pdf). 2008 revision. United Nations. . Retrieved 2009-03-12. NB: The preliminary results of the National population census in Guinea-Bissau put the figure at 1,449,230, according to email information by the Instituto Nacional de Estudos e Pesquisa, Bissau.

[3] "Guinea-Bissau" (http://www.imf.org/external/pubs/ft/weo/2011/01/weodata/weorept.aspx?sy=2008&ey=2011&scsm=1&ssd=1& sort=country&ds=.&br=1&c=654&s=NGDPD,NGDPDPC,PPPGDP,PPPPC,LP&grp=0&a=&pr.x=55&pr.y=12). International Monetary Fund. . Retrieved 2011-04-21.

[4] Jihan El Tahri. (2007). *Cuba! Africa! Revolution!* (http://www.bbc.co.uk/bbcfour/documentaries/storyville/). BBC Television. Event occurs at 50:00-60:00. . Retrieved 2007-05-02.

[5] "Army man wins G Bissau election" (http://news.bbc.co.uk/1/hi/world/africa/4723627.stm). London. 28 July 2005. . Retrieved January 5, 2010.

[6] Balde, Assimo (Monday, 24 November 2008). "Coup attempt fails in Guinea-Bissau" (http://www.independent.co.uk/news/world/africa/ coup-attempt-fails-in-guineabissau-1032371.html). London: The Independent UK independent.co.uk. . Retrieved 2010-06-28.

[7] "Já foi escolhida a data para a realização das eleições presidenciais entecipadas" (http://www.bissaudigital.com/noticias. php?idnoticia=3609). Bissaudigital.com. 2009-04-01. . Retrieved 2010-06-26.

[8] Assimo Balde, "Soldiers put Guinea-Bissau PM under house arrest" (http://www.google.com/hostednews/ap/article/ ALeqM5gJesugYieOra7PfjTwVraPl9gg_wD9EQGRQG2), Associated Press, 1 April 2010.

[9] EU pull-out hits Guinea-Bissau reforms (http://www.bbc.co.uk/news/world-europe-10871260) *BBC*

[10] ANGOP, "Angolan military mission in Guinea Bissau launched", 21 March 2010 (http://www.portalangop.co.ao/motix/en_us/noticias/ politica/2011/2/12/Angolan-military-mission-Guinea-Bissau-launched,1f4c18f5-dec7-4c79-a9ae-4645d75a78b8.html)

[11] Reuters, "Angola to send military, police officals [*sic*] to Bissau", 21 Sep 2010 (http://af.reuters.com/article/guineaBissauNews/ idAFLDE6881F820100909)

[12] Africa - new front in drugs war (http://news.bbc.co.uk/2/hi/africa/6274590.stm) *BBC*

[13] G Bissau drugs sanctions threat (http://news.bbc.co.uk/2/hi/africa/7650063.stm) *BBC*

[14] US names two Guinea-Bissau military men 'drug kingpins' (http://news.bbc.co.uk/2/hi/africa/8610924.stm) *BBC*

[15] (http://www.news.com.au/dailytelegraph/story/0,22049,25128786-5012772,00.html)

[16] Elections, Guinea-Bissau (May 27, 2009). "On the Radio Waves in Guinea-Bissau" (http://beforeproject.org/2009/05/ on-the-radio-waves-in-guinea-bissau/). swisspeace. . Retrieved 7 February 2010.

[17] BBC news "New Senegal record cocaine haul" (http://news.bbc.co.uk/1/hi/world/africa/6260708.stm). London. 2 July 2007. BBC news. Retrieved January 5, 2010.

[18] Sullivan, Kevin (25 May 2008). "Route of Evil: How a tiny West African nation became a key smuggling hub for Colombian cocaine, and the price it is paying" (http://www.washingtonpost.com/wp-dyn/content/article/2008/05/24/AR2008052401676.html). *Washington Post.* .

[19] "OHADA.com: The business law portal in Africa" (http://www.ohada.com/index.php). . Retrieved 2009-03-22

[20] CIA the World Factbook (https://www.cia.gov/library/publications/the-world-factbook/geos/pu.html)

[21] "Guinea-Bissau" (http://www.britannica.com/EBchecked/topic/248853/Guinea-Bissau/), *Encyclopædia Britannica*

[22] The WHO identified only 78 physicians in the entire Guinea-Bissau health workforce in 2009 data. ("Health workforce, infrastructure, essential medicines" (http://www.who.int/whosis/whostat/EN_WHS10_Part2.pdf) (PDF). 2010. p. 118. .) And the World Bank estimates that Guinea-Bissau had 1,575,446 residents in 2008 (http://www.google.com/publicdata?ds=wb-wdi&met=sp_pop_totl& idim=country:GNB&dl=en&hl=en&q=guinea-bissau+population). At the current rate of population growth there would have been about

1.61 million people in the country by 2009, of which 0.0048% are known to be medical doctors involved in patient care. The WHO estimate an average of about 20 per 100,000 across Africa, but reports a density per 10,000 population of **<0.5** in its *Physicians data covering the period to 2009*. However, Guinea-Bissau has an unusually high ratio of nursing staff to doctors: including nurses and midwives, there are 64 medical professionals per 100,000 Bissau-Guineans

[23] The WHO estimates that there were 188 physicians working in the entire country as of 2007 ("Health workforce, infrastructure, essential medicines" (http://www.who.int/whosis/whostat/EN_WHS09_Table6.pdf). 2009. p. 98. .). And The World Bank estimates that Guinea-Bissau had 1,541,040 residents in 2007 ("Midyear estimates of the resident population" (http://www.google.com/ publicdata?ds=wb-wdi&met=sp_pop_totl&idim=country:GNB&dl=en&hl=en&q=guinea-bissau+population). 2010. .). So, about 0.0122% of the permanent population were known to be medical doctors involved in patient care, as of 2007.

[24] The WHO estimates a 1.8% HIV-infection rate from 2007 data among 15- to 49-year old Bissau-Guineans - see statistics on page 65 of: "2. Cause-specific mortality and morbidity" (http://www.who.int/whosis/whostat/EN_WHS10_Part2.pdf) (PDF). WHO. 2010. .. (The section's introduction describes estimation methodology).

[25] As of 2008, only 20% of HIV-infected mothers or sufferers with advanced cases had anti-retroviral drug access, see: "Health service coverage" (http://www.who.int/whosis/whostat/EN_WHS10_Part2.pdf). WHO. 2010. p. 91. .. Coverage in the general population is lower.

[26] "Selected infectious diseases" (http://www.who.int/whosis/whostat/EN_WHS10_Part2.pdf). WHO. 2010. p. 76. . Retrieved 2010-06-09. - 148,542 reported cases in 2008.)

[27] According to the 2010 WHO report, the latest Malaria mortality rate per 100,000 Bissau-Guineans (180) is substantially greater than that for AIDS (65). ("Cause-specific mortality and morbidity" (http://www.who.int/whosis/whostat/EN_WHS10_Part2.pdf). WHO. 2010. p. 64. . Retrieved 2010-06-09.) Among children younger than 5, Malaria is nine times more deadly (p. 65).

[28] "Global Health Indicators: 4. Health service coverage" (http://www.who.int/whosis/whostat/EN_WHS10_Part2.pdf). WHO. 2010. p. 91. .

[29] http://www.unfpa.org/sowmy/report/home.html

[30] "The State Of The World's Midwifery" (http://www.unfpa.org/sowmy/report/home.html). United Nations Population Fund. Accessed August 2011. .

[31] "Bureau of International Labor Affairs (ILAB) - U.S. Department of Labor" (http://www.dol.gov/ilab/media/reports/iclp/tda2001/ guinea-bissau.htm). Dol.gov. . Retrieved 2010-06-26.

[32] http://hdrstats.undp.org/2008/countries/country_fact_sheets/cty_fs_GNB.html

[33] The latter is maintained by Cuba and functions in different cities.

[34] "Global Health Indicators: Mortality and burden of disease" (http://www.who.int/whosis/whostat/EN_WHS10_Part2.pdf). 2010. p. 50. .. *Healthy* life expectancy at birth was 42, and the probability of dying between a live-birth and age 5 was 19.5% (down from 24% in 1990, p.51).

Ⓒ *This article incorporates public domain material from websites or documents* (https://www.cia.gov/library/ publications/the-world-factbook/index.html) *of the CIA World Factbook.*

Sources

* Joshua B. Forrest, *Lineages of State Fragility. Rural Civil Society in Guinea-Bissau* (Ohio University Press/James Currey Ltd., 2003).
* Richard Andrew Lobban, Jr. and Peter Karibe Mendy, *Historical Dictionary of the Republic of Guinea-Bissau*, third edition (Scarecrow Press, 1997) ISBN 0-8108-3226-7 (includes extensive bibliography)

External links

Government

* Official government website (http://www.gov.gw)
* Chief of State and Cabinet Members (https://www.cia.gov/library/publications/world-leaders-1/ world-leaders-g/guinea-bissau.html)
* Constitution of the Republic of Guinea-Bissau (http://www.constitutionnet.org/files/Guinea-Bissau Constitution.pdf)

General information

* Link collection related to Guinea-Bissau on bolama.net (http://www.bolama.net/pt/guine-bissau-links.html)
* Country Profile (http://news.bbc.co.uk/1/hi/world/africa/country_profiles/1043287.stm) from BBC News

- Guinea-Bissau (https://www.cia.gov/library/publications/the-world-factbook/geos/pu.html) entry at *The World Factbook*
- Guinea-Bissau (http://ucblibraries.colorado.edu/govpubs/for/guineabissau.htm) from *UCB Libraries GovPubs*
- Guinea-Bissau (http://www.britannica.com/EBchecked/topic/248853/Guinea-Bissau/) at *Encyclopædia Britannica*
- Guinea-Bissau (http://www.dmoz.org/Regional/Africa/Guinea-Bissau/) at the Open Directory Project
- Wikimedia Atlas of Guinea-Bissau
- Before Project has a lot of information on the history of political violence and how it has been overcome (http://beforeproject.org/2009/05/on-the-radio-waves-in-guinea-bissau/)

News media

- news headline links (http://allafrica.com/guineabissau/) from AllAfrica.com

Tourism

- Guinea-Bissau travel guide from Wikitravel

Health

- The State of the World's Midwifery - Guinea-Bissau Country Profile (http://www.unfpa.org/sowmy/resources/docs/country_info/profile/en_GuineaBissau_SoWMy_Profile.pdf)

bjn:Guinea-Bissau gag:Gvineya Bissau mrj:Гвиней-Бисау

Sierra Leone

Republic of Sierra Leone	
Sierra Leone	
Motto: "Unity, Freedom, Justice"	
Anthem: *High We Exalt Thee, Realm of the Free*	

Location of Sierra Leone(dark blue)

— in Africa(light blue & dark grey)
— in the African Union(light blue) — [Legend]

Capital (and largest city)	Freetown 8°29.067′N 13°14.067′W
Official language(s)	English
Demonym	Sierra Leonean
Government	Constitutional republic
- President	Ernest Bai Koroma (APC)
- Vice President	Alhaji Samuel Sam-Sumana (APC)
- Speaker of Parliament	Abel Nathaniel Bankole Stronge (APC)
- Chief Justice	Umu Hawa Tejan-Jalloh
Legislature	House of Parliament of Sierra Leone
Independence	
- from the United Kingdom	27 April 1961
- Republic declared	19 April 1971
Area	

-	Total	71,740 km^2 (119th)
		27,699 sq mi
-	Water (%)	1.1
Population		
-	July 2010 estimate	6.4 million [1] [2] (103rd[1])
-	Density	79.4/km^2 (114th[1])
		205.6/sq mi
GDP (PPP)		2009 estimate
-	Total	$4.585 billion[3]
-	Per capita	$759[3]
GDP (nominal)		2009 estimate
-	Total	$1.877 billion[3]
-	Per capita	$311[3]
Gini (2003)		62.9 (high)
HDI (2007)		▲ 0.365 (low) (158th)
Currency		Leone (SLL)
Time zone		GMT (UTC+0)
Drives on the		right
ISO 3166 code		SL
Internet TLD		.sl
Calling code		232

[1] Rank based on 2007 figures.

Sierra Leone ◀ /siːˈɛrəliːˈoʊn/ (Krio: *Salone*), officially the **Republic of Sierra Leone**, is a country in West Africa. It is bordered by Guinea to the north and east, Liberia to the southeast, and the Atlantic Ocean to the west and southwest. Sierra Leone covers a total area of 71740 km^2 (27699 sq mi)[4] and has a population of 6.4 million.[5] It was a colony under the auspices of the Sierra Leone Company from March 11, 1792 until it became a British colony in 1808. Sierra Leone has a tropical climate, with a diverse environment ranging from savannah to rainforests.[6] Sierra Leone is divided into four geographical regions: the Northern Province, Eastern Province, Southern Province and the Western Area; which are further divided into fourteen districts. Freetown is the capital, largest city and economic and financial center. The other major cities are Bo, Kenema, Koidu Town and Makeni.

Sierra Leone is now a constitutional republic, with a directly elected president and a unicameral legislature, known as the House of Parliament. The president is the head of state and the Head of government. The Judiciary of Sierra Leone is independent of the executive and the legislature and consist of the Supreme Court, Court of Appeals, High Court of Justice and magistrate courts. Judges of the Supreme Court, Court of Appeals and High Court of Justice are appointed by the president and subject to the approval by parliament. Thirteen of the country's fourteen district has its own directly elected local government called district council, headed by a Council Chairman. The country's six minicipalities of Freetown, Bo, Kenema, Koidu Town, Makeni and the island of Bonthe in turn have directly elected city councils, headed by mayors.

The country has relied on mining, especially diamonds, for its economic base; it is among the top 10 diamond producing nations in the world, and mineral exports remain the main foreign currency earner. Sierra Leone is also among the largest producers of titanium and bauxite, and a major producer of gold. The country has one of the world's largest deposits of rutile. Sierra Leone is also home to the third largest natural harbour in the world; where shipping from all over the globe berth at Freetown's famous Queen Elizabeth II Quay. Despite this natural wealth, over 70% of its people live in poverty [7].

Sierra Leone is home to fifteen ethnic groups, each with its own language and customs. The two largest and most influential are the Mende and Temne. The Mende are predominantly found in South-Eastern Sierra Leone; the Temne likewise predominate in the Northern Sierra Leone. Although English is the official language of Sierra Leone, the Krio language (derived from English and several indigenous African languages) is the most widely spoken language in virtually all parts of Sierra Leone. The Krio language is spoken by 97%[8] of the country's population and unites all the different ethnic groups, especially in their trade and interaction with each other.[9] Sierra Leone is a predominantly Muslim nation, though with a large Christian minority. Sierra Leone is ranked as one of the most religiously tolerant nations in the world [10] [11][12]. People are often married across tribal and religious boundaries. Muslims and Christians collaborate and interact with each other peacefully.[10]. Religious violence is extremely rare in the country.

Between 1991 and 2002 the Sierra Leone Civil War devastated the country leaving more than 75,000 people dead, much of the country's infrastructure and over two million people displaced in neighbouring countries; mainly to Guinea, which was home to more than six hundred thousand Sierra Leonean refugees [13]. The war was resolved in 2002 after the Nigerian-led ECOMOG troops were heavily reinforced by a British force spearheaded by 1st Bn The Parachute Regiment, supported by the British Royal Navy The arrival of this force resulted in the defeat of rebel forces and restored the civilian government elected in 1998. On January 18, 2002 President Ahmad Tejan Kabbah declared the civil war officially over [14]. Since then the country has re-established a functioning democracy.

Early inhabitants of Sierra Leone included the Sherbro, Temne and Limba peoples, and later the Mende,[15] who knew the country as Romarong, and the Kono who settled in the east of the country.[16] In 1462, it was visited by the Portuguese explorer Pedro da Cintra, who dubbed it Serra de Leão, meaning "Lion Mountains".[17] [18] Sierra Leone later became an important centre of the transatlantic trade in slaves until March 11, 1792 when Freetown was founded by the Sierra Leone Company as a home for formerly enslaved African Americans.[19] In 1808, Freetown became a British Crown Colony, and in 1896, and the interior of the country became a British Protectorate;[16] in 1961, the two regions combined and gained independence.

History

Early history

Archaeological finds show that Sierra Leone has been inhabited continuously for at least 2,500 years,[20] populated by successive movements from other parts of Africa.[21] The use of iron was introduced to Sierra Leone by the 9th century, and by AD 1000 agriculture was being practiced by coastal tribes.[22] Sierra Leone's dense tropical rainforest largely protected it from the influence of any pre-colonial African empires[23] and from further Islamic influence of the Mali Empire, the Islamic faith however became common in the 18th century.[24]

Fragments of prehistoric pottery from Kamabai Rock Shelter

European contacts within Sierra Leone were among the first in West Africa. In 1462, Portuguese explorer Pedro da Cintra mapped the hills surrounding what is now Freetown Harbour, naming shaped formation *Serra de Leão* (Portuguese for Lion Mountains).[18] The Italian rendering of this geographic formation is *Sierra Leone*, which became the country's name.

Soon after Portuguese traders arrived at the harbour and by 1495 a fort that acted as a trading post had been built.[25] The Portuguese were joined by the Dutch and French; all of them using Sierra Leone as a trading point for slaves.[26] In 1562, the English joined the trade in human beings when Sir John Hawkins shipped 300 enslaved people, acquired 'by the sword and partly by other means', to the new colonies in America.[27]

An 1835 illustration of liberated Africans arriving in Sierra Leone.

Early Colonies

In 1787 a settlement was founded by in Sierra Leone in what was called the "Province of Freedom". A number of "Black Poor" arrived off the coast of Sierra Leone on 15 May 1787, accompanied by some English tradesmen. Many of the "black poor" were African Americans, who had been given their freedom after seeking refuge with the British Army during the American Revolution, but also included other West Indian, African and Asian inhabitants of London. After establishing Granville Town,

The colony of Freetown in 1856.

disease and hostility from the indigenous people eliminated the first group of colonists and destroyed their settlement. A second Granville Town was established by 64 remaining colonists.[28]

Through the impetus of Thomas Peters, the Sierra Leone Company was established to relocate 1,196 black Americans, most of whom had escaped enslavement in the United States by seeking protection with the British Army during the American Revolution. They had been given land in Nova Scotia and a few had died from the harsh winters there. These colonists built the second (and only permanent) Colony of Sierra Leone and the settlement of Freetown on March 11, 1792. In Sierra Leone they were called the Nova Scotian Settlers or 'Nova Scotians' but were commonly known as the *Settlers*. The Settlers built Freetown and introduced architectural styles from the American South as well as Western fashion and American courtesy. In the 1790s, the Settlers voted for the first time in elections, as did women.[29] The Sierra Leone Company refused to allow the settlers to take freehold of the land. Some of the Settlers revolted in 1799. The revolt was only put down by the arrival of over 500 Jamaican Maroons, who also arrived via Nova Scotia. In 1800, Jamaican Maroons from Trelawny Town, Jamaica were settled via Nova Scotia.

After sixteen years of the running the Colony, the Sierra Leone Company was formed into the African Institution. The Institution met in 1807 to achieve more success by focusing on bettering the local economy, but it was constantly split between those British who meant to inspire local entrepreneurs and those with interest in the Macauley & Babington Company which held the (British) monopoly on Sierra Leone trade.[30]

Beginning in 1808 (following the abolition of the slave trade in 1807), thousands of formerly enslaved Africans were liberated in Freetown. Most of these Liberated Africans or 'Recaptives' chose to remain in Sierra Leone. Cut off from their homes and traditions, the Liberated Africans assimilated the Western styles of Settlers and Maroons and built a flourishing trade of flowers and beads on the West African coast. These returned Africans were from many areas of Africa, but principally the west coast. During the 19th century many black Americans, Americo Liberian 'refugees', and particularly West Indians immigrated and settled in Freetown creating a new ethnicity called the Krio.

Colonial era

In the early 20th century, Freetown served as the residence of the British governor who also ruled the Gold Coast (now Ghana) and the Gambia settlements. Sierra Leone also served as the educational centre of British West Africa. Fourah Bay College, established in 1827, rapidly became a magnet for English-speaking Africans on the West Coast. For more than a century, it was the only European-style university in western Sub-Saharan Africa.

During Sierra Leone's colonial history, indigenous people mounted several unsuccessful revolts against British rule. The most notable was the Hut Tax war of 1898. The Hut Tax War consisted of a Northern front, led by Bai Bureh, and Southern front that were sparked at different times and for different reasons. Bureh's fighters had the advantage over the vastly more powerful British for several months of the war. Hundreds of British troops and hundreds of Bureh's fighters were killed.[31] Bai Bureh was finally captured on 11 November 1898 and sent into exile in the Gold Coast (now Ghana), while 96 of his comrades were hanged by the British.

Bai Bureh, leader of the 1898 rebellion against British rule

The defeat in the Hut Tax war ended large scale organised resistance to colonialism; however resistance continued throughout the colonial period in the form of intermittent rioting and chaotic labour disturbances. Riots in 1955 and 1956 involved "many tens of thousands" of natives in the protectorate.[32]

One notable event in 1935 was the granting of a monopoly on mineral mining to the Sierra Leone Selection Trust run by De Beers, which was scheduled to last 98 years.

In 1924, Sierra Leone was divided into a Colony and a Protectorate, with separate and different political systems constitutionally defined for each. Antagonism between the two entities escalated to a heated debate in 1947, when proposals were introduced to provide for a single political

1919 etching originally captioned: "BRITISH EXPEDITIONARY FORCE PREPARING TO EMBARK AT FREETOWN TO ATTACK THE GERMAN CAMEROONS, THE MAIN OBJECT OF THE ATTACK BEING THE PORT OF DUALA. AUXILIARY NATIVE TROOPS WERE FREELY USED IN AFRICAN WARFARE."

system for both the Colony and the Protectorate. Most of the proposals came from the Protectorate. The Krio, led by Isaac Wallace-Johnson, opposed the proposals, the main effect of which would have been to diminish their political power. It was due to the astute politics of Sir Milton Margai, who was the son of a Creole man by the name of Tu-borku Metzeger, that the educated Protectorate elite was won over to join forces with the paramount chiefs in the face of Krio intransigence. Later, Sir Milton [whose real family name was Tu Borku Metzeger] used the same skills to win over opposition leaders and moderate Krio elements for the achievement of independence.

In November 1951, Sir Milton Margai oversaw the drafting of a new constitution, which united the separate Colonial and Protectorate legislatures and—-most importantly—provided a framework for decolonization.[33] In 1953, Sierra Leone was granted local ministerial powers, and Sir Milton Margai, was elected Chief Minister of Sierra Leone.[33] The new constitution ensured Sierra Leone a parliamentary system within the Commonwealth of Nations.[33] In May 1957, Sierra Leone held its first parliamentary election. The SLPP, which was then the most popular political party in the colony of Sierra Leone, won the majority of the seats in Parliament. Margai was also re-elected as Chief Minister by a landslide.

Margai led the Sierra Leonean delegation at the constitutional conferences that were held with British Colonial Secretary Iain Macleod in London in 1960. All members of the Sierra Leonean delegation were prominent and well-respected politicians including Sir Milton's younger brother Sir Albert Margai, John Karefa-Smart, Lamina Sankoh, Kande Bureh, Sir Banja Tejan-Sie, Ella Koblo Gulama, Amadu Wurie, Mohamed Sanusi Mustapha and Eustace Henry Taylor Cummings. Two notable absentees from the delegation were Siaka Stevens, the leader of the opposition APC, and the veteran Creole politician Isaac Wallace-Johnson who were placed under house arrest in Freetown, charged with disrupting the Independence movement.[34]

Early independence (1961 - 1991)

On the 27 April 1961 Sierra Leone became politically independent of Great Britain. It retained a parliamentary system of government and was a member of the British Commonwealth of Nations. Sierra Leone's first general election was held in May 1962 with Sierra Leone People's Party (SLPP) being elected and Sir Milton Margai becoming prime minister.[35] [36] The years just after independence were prosperous with money from mineral resources being used for development and the founding of Njala University.[36] Upon Sir Milton's death in 1964, his half-brother, Sir Albert Margai, was appointed as Prime Minister. He proved unpopular and resorted to increasingly authoritarian actions in response to protests, including enacted several laws against the

APC political rally in Kabala outside the home of supporters of the rival SLPP in 1968

opposition All People's Congress (APC) and attempting to establish a single-party state.[37] The APC, with leader Siaka Stevens, won the 1967 general election. Within a week the army had created a military government.[36] [38] In April 1968 parts of the military revolted in a "counter-coup" allowing the APC and Stevens to take power.[39]

Stevens ruled for the next 18 years, a period of political violence, government centralisation and dictatorship, and economic deterioration.[36] [40] In November 1968 a state of emergency was declared after provincial disturbances, and in March 1971 the government survived an unsuccessful military coup. In April 1971 a republican constitution was adopted under which Stevens became President. In 1972 by-elections the opposition SLPP complained of intimidation and procedural obstruction by the APC and militia. These problems became so severe that it boycotted the 1973 general election; as a result the APC won 84 of the 85 elected seats.[41] In July 1974, the government uncovered an alleged military coup plot. As in 1971, the leaders of were tried and executed. In 1977, student demonstrations against the government disrupted Sierra Leone politics. A general election was called later that year in which corruption was again endemic; the APC won 74 seats and the SLPP 15.

Siaka Stevens retired in November 1985 and was succeeded by his favoured candidate head of the Sierra Leone Armed Forces, Major General Joseph Saidu Momoh. Joseph Saidu Momoh was sworn in Freetown on 28 November 1985 with Francis Minah as Vice president. A one party parliamentary election between APC members was held in May, 1986. President Momoh's strong links with the army and his verbal attacks on corruption earned him much needed initial support among Sierra Leoneans. With the lack of new faces in the new APC cabinet under president Momoh and the return of many of the old faces from Stevens government, criticisms soon arose that Momoh was simply perpetuating the rule of Stevens. The next couple of years under the Momoh administration were characterised by corruption, which Momoh defused by sacking several senior cabinet ministers. To formalise his war against corruption, President Momoh announced a "Code of Conduct for Political Leaders and Public Servants." After an alleged attempt to overthrow President Momoh in March 1987, more than 60 senior government officials were arrested, including Vice-President Francis Minah, who was removed from office, convicted for plotting the coup, and executed by hanging in 1989 along with 5 others.

Multi-party constitution and Revolutionary United Front rebellion (1991 to present)

Between 1991 and 2002 civil war devastated the country leaving more than 50,000 people dead and much of the country's infrastructure destroyed.[43] Civil war broke out, mainly due to government corruption and mismanagement of diamond resources and abuse of power by various governments since independence from Britain (Truth and Reconciliation Commission's Report). The brutal civil war going on in neighbouring Liberia played an undeniable role in the outbreak of fighting in Sierra Leone. Charles Taylor—then leader of the National Patriotic Front of Liberia—reportedly helped form the Revolutionary United Front (RUF) under the command of former Sierra Leonean army corporal Foday Saybana Sankoh, an ethnic Temne from Tonkolili District in Northern Sierra Leone. Sankoh was a British trained former

A school in Koindu destroyed during the Civil War, in total 1,270 primary schools were destroyed in the War.[42]

army corporal who had also undergone guerrilla training in Libya. Taylor's aim was for the RUF to attack the bases of Nigerian dominated peacekeeping troops in Freetown who were opposed to his rebel movement in Liberia. In 2003 Foday Sankoh was indicted by the Special Court for Sierra Leone for war crimes and crimes against humanity and died under UN custody before the trials could be concluded. Charles Taylor, the former president of Liberia, is currently in the Hague at the Special Court for Sierra Leone (SCSL), where he faces charges of war crimes and crimes against humanity for crimes allegedly committed by Sankoh's RUF in Sierra Leone.

The RUF, led by Sankoh and backed by Taylor, launched its first attack in villages in Kailahun District in Eastern Sierra Leone from Liberia on 23 March 1991. The government of Sierra Leone, overwhelmed by a crumbling economy and corruption, as well as a demoralised army, was unable to put up significant resistance against the incursion of the RUF. Within a month of entering Sierra Leone from Liberia, the RUF controlled much of Eastern Sierra Leone, including the cash crop production areas of Kailahun and the government diamond mines in Kono District. Forced recruitment of child soldiers was also an early feature of the rebel strategy.

In October 1999, the United Nations agreed to send peacekeepers to help restore order and disarm the rebels. The first of the 6,000-member force began arriving in December, and the UN Security Council voted in February 2000 to increase the force to 11,000, and later to 13,000. But in May, when nearly all Nigerian forces had left and UN forces were trying to disarm the RUF in eastern Sierra Leone, Sankoh's forces clashed with the UN troops, and some 500 peacekeepers were taken hostage as the peace accord effectively collapsed. The hostage crisis resulted in more fighting between the RUF and the government as UN troops launched Operation Khukri to end the siege. The Operation was successful with Indian and British Special Forces being the main contingents.

The situation in the country deteriorated to such an extent that British troops were deployed in Operation Palliser, originally simply to evacuate foreign nationals. However, the British exceeded their original mandate, and took full military action to finally defeat the rebels and restore order. The British were the catalyst for the ceasefire that ended the civil war. Elements of the British Army, together with administrators and politicians, remain in Sierra Leone to this day, helping train the armed forces, improve the infrastructure of the country and administer financial and material aid. Tony Blair, the Prime Minister of Britain at the time of the British intervention, is regarded as a hero by the people of Sierra Leone, many of whom are keen for more British involvement. Sierra Leoneans have been described as "The World's Most Resilient People".[44]

Between 1991 and 2001, about 50,000 people were killed in Sierra Leone's civil war. Hundreds of thousands of people were forced from their homes and many became refugees in Guinea and Liberia. In 2001, UN forces moved into rebel-held areas and began to disarm rebel soldiers. By January 2002, the war was declared over. In May 2002, Kabbah was re-elected president. By 2004, the disarmament process was complete. Also in 2004, a UN-backed war crimes court began holding trials of senior leaders from both sides of the war. In December 2005, UN peacekeeping forces pulled out of Sierra Leone.

In August 2007, Sierra Leone held presidential and parliamentary elections. However, no presidential candidate won the 50% plus one vote majority stipulated in the constitution on the first round of voting. A runoff election was held in September 2007, and Ernest Bai Koroma, the candidate of the APC and ethnically a half Limba and half Temne from the north was elected president.

By 2007, there had been an increase in the number of drug cartels, many from Colombia, using Sierra Leone as a base to ship drugs on to Europe.[29] It was feared that this might lead to increased corruption and violence and turn the country, like neighbouring Guinea-Bissau, into a narco state. However, the new government of president Koroma quickly amended the laws against drug trafficking in the country, updating the existing legislation from those inherited at independence in 1961, to address the international concerns, increasing punishment for offenders both in terms of higher, if not prohibitive, fines, lengthier prison terms and provision for possible extradition of offenders wanted elsewhere, including to the United States.

Geography and climate

Sierra Leone is located on the west coast of Africa, lying mostly between latitudes 7° and 10°N (a small area is south of 7°), and longitudes 10° and 14°W.

The country is bordered by Guinea to the north and northeast, Liberia to the south and southeast, and the Atlantic Ocean to the west.[45]

Sierra Leone has a total area of 71740 km^2 (27699 sq mi), divided into a land area of 71620 km^2 (27653 sq mi) and water of 120 km^2 (46 sq mi).[8] The country has four distinct geographical regions. In eastern Sierra Leone the plateau is interspersed with high mountains, where Mount Bintumani reaches 1948 m (6391 ft), the highest point in the country. The upper part of the drainage basin of the Moa River is located in the south of this region.

Satellite image of Sierra Leone

The centre of the country is a region of lowland plains, containing forests, bush and farmland,[45] that occupies about 43% of Sierra Leone's land area. The northern section of this has been categorised by the World Wildlife Fund as part of the Guinean forest-savanna mosaic ecoregion, while the south is rain-forested plains and farmland. In the west Sierra Leone has some 400 km (249 mi) of Atlantic coastline, giving it both bountiful marine resources and attractive tourist potential. The coast has areas of low-lying Guinean mangroves swamp. The national capital Freetown sits on a coastal peninsula, situated next to the Sierra Leone Harbour, the world's third largest natural harbour.

The climate is tropical, with two seasons determining the agricultural cycle: the rainy season from May to November, and a dry season from December to May, which includes harmattan, when cool, dry winds blow in off the Sahara Desert and the night-time temperature can be as low as 16 °C (60.8 °F). The average temperature is 26 °C (78.8 °F) and varies from around 26 °C (78.8 °F) to 36 °C (96.8 °F) during the year.[46] [47]

Environment

Logging, mining, slash and burn, and deforestation for land conversion - such as cattle grazing - have dramatically diminished forested land in Sierra Leone since the 1980s. Correspondingly the habitat for the African Wild Dog, *Lycaon pictus*, has been decreased, such that this canid is deemed to have been extirpated in Sierra Leone.[48]

Until 2002, Sierra Leone lacked a forest management system due to the civil war that caused tens of thousands of deaths. Deforestation rates have increased 7.3% since the end of the civil war.[49] On paper, 55 protected areas covered 4.5% of Sierra Leone as of 2003. The country has 2,090 known species of higher plants, 147 mammals, 626 birds, 67 reptiles, 35 amphibians, and 99 fish species.[49]

The Environmental Justice Foundation has documented how the number of illegal fishing vessels in Sierra Leone's waters has multiplied in recent years. The amount of illegal fishing has significantly depleted fish stocks, depriving local fishing communities of an important resource for survival. The situation is particularly serious as fishing provides the only source of income for many communities in a country still recovering from over a decade of civil war.[50]

In June 2005, the Royal Society for the Protection of Birds (RSPB) and Bird Life International agreed to support a conservation-sustainable development project in the Gola Forest in south eastern Sierra Leone,[51] an important surviving fragment of rainforest in Sierra Leone.

Government and politics

Sierra Leone is a constitutional republic with a directly elected president and a unicameral legislature. The current system of government in Sierra Leone, established under the 1991 Constitution, is modelled on the following structure of government: the Legislature, the Executive and the Judiciary.[52]

Within the confines of the 1991 Constitution, supreme legislative powers are vested in Parliament, which is the law making body of the nation. Supreme executive authority rests in the president and members of his cabinet and judicial power with the judiciary of which the Chief Justice is head.

The president is the head of state, the head of government and the commander-in-chief of the Sierra Leone Armed Forces and the Sierra Leone Police. The president appoints and heads a cabinet of ministers, which must be approved by the Parliament. The president is elected by popular vote to a maximum of two five-year terms. The president is the highest and most influential position within the government of Sierra Leone.

Ernest Bai Koroma, current president of Sierra Leone

To be elected president of Sierra Leone, a candidate must gain at least 55% of the vote. If no candidate gets 55%, there is to be a second-round runoff between the top two candidates.

The current president of Sierra Leone is Ernest Bai Koroma, who was sworn in on 17 September 2007, shortly after being declared the winner of a tense run-off election over the incumbent Vice president, Solomon Berewa of the Sierra Leone People's Party (SLPP).[53]

Next to the president is the Vice president, who is the second-highest ranking government official in the executive branch of the Sierra Leone Government. As designated by the Sierra Leone Constitution, the vice president is to become the new president of Sierra Leone upon the death, resignation, or removal of the president by parliament and to assume the Presidency temporarily while the president is otherwise temporarily unable to fulfil his or her duties. The vice president is elected jointly with the president as his or her running mate. Sierra Leone's current vice president is Samuel Sam-Sumana, sworn in on 17 September 2007.

The Sierra Leone Supreme Court in the capital Freetown, the highest and most powerful court in the country

The Parliament of Sierra Leone is unicameral, with 124 seats. Each of the country's fourteen districts is represented in parliament. 112 members are elected concurrently with the presidential elections; the other 12 seats are filled by paramount chiefs from each of the country's 12 administrative districts.

The current parliament in the August 2007 Parliamentary elections is made up of three political parties. The most recent parliamentary elections were held on 11 August 2007. The All People's Congress (APC), won 59 of 112 parliamentary seats; the Sierra Leone People's Party (SLPP) won 43; and the People's Movement for Democratic Change (PMDC) won 10. To be qualified as Member of Parliament, the person must be a citizen of Sierra Leone, must be at least 21 years old, must be able to speak, read and write the English language with a degree of proficiency to enable him to actively take part in proceedings in Parliament; and must not have any criminal conviction.[52]

Since independence in 1961, Sierra Leone's politics has been dominated by two major political parties, the Sierra Leone People's Party (SLPP), and the ruling All People's Congress (APC), although other minor political parties have also existed but with no significant supports.

The judicial power of Sierra Leone is vested in the judiciary, headed by the Chief Justice and comprising the Sierra Leone Supreme Court, which is the highest court in the country and its ruling therefore cannot be appealed; High Court of Justice; the Court of Appeal; the magistrate courts; and traditional courts in rural villages. The president appoints and parliament approves Justices for the three courts. The Judiciary have jurisdiction in all civil and criminal matters throughout the country. The current Sierra Leone's Chief Justice is Umu Hawa Tejan Jalloh, who was appointed by President Ernest Bai Koroma and took office on 25 January 2008 upon her confirmation by parliament. She is the first woman in the history of Sierra Leone to hold such position.[54]

Foreign relations

The Sierra Leone Ministry of Foreign Affairs and International Relations, headed by Minister of Foreign Affairs Zainab Hawa Bangura is responsible for foreign policy of Sierra Leone. Sierra Leone has diplomatic relations that include China, Libya, Iran, and Cuba. Sierra Leone has good relations with the West, including the United States and has maintained historical ties with the United Kingdom and other former British colonies through membership of the Commonwealth of Nations.[55] The United Kingdom has played a major role in providing aid to the former colony, together with administrative help and military training since intervening to end the Civil War in 2000.

Embassy of Sierra Leone in Washington, D.C.

Former President Siaka Stevens' government had sought closer relations with other West African countries under the Economic Community of West African States (ECOWAS) a policy continued by the current. Sierra Leone, along with Liberia and Guinea form the Mano River Union (MRU) primarily designed to implement development projects and promote regional economic integration between the three countries.[56]

Sierra Leone is also a member of the United Nations and its specialized agencies, the African Union, the African Development Bank (AFDB), the Organisation of Islamic Cooperation (OIC), and the Non-Aligned Movement (NAM).[57] Sierra Leone is also a member of the International Criminal Court with a Bilateral Immunity Agreement of protection for the US military (as covered under Article 98).

The Office of National Security plays an important security coordination role, including in the leadup to the 2007 elections.[58]

Provinces and districts

The Republic of Sierra Leone is composed of four regions the Northern Province, Southern Province, the Eastern Province and the Western Area. The first three provinces are further divided into 12 districts, and the districts are further divided into 149 chiefdoms. The Local Government Act 2004 designated units of government called localities each of which would have a council to exercise authority and carry out functions at a local level.[59] [60] There are 13 district councils, one for each of the 12 districts and one for the Western Area Rural, and six municipalities each with a council, Freetown, Bo, Bonthe, Kenema, Koidu and Makeni.[59]

1 - Western Area Urban
2 - Western Area Rural

The 12 districts and 2 areas of Sierra Leone.

District	Capital	!Area km²	Province	Population (2004 census)[61]	Population (2008 estimates)
Bombali District	Makeni	7,985	Northern Province	408,390	424,100[62]
Koinadugu District	Kabala	12,121		265,758	
Port Loko District	Port Loko	5,719		455,746	483,752[63]
Tonkolili District	Magburaka	7,003		347,197	370,425[64]
Kambia District	Kambia	3,108		270,462	299,725[65]
Kenema District	Kenema	6,053	Eastern Province	497,948	522,656[66]
Kono District	Koidu Town	5,641		335,401	
Kailahun District	Kailahun	3,859		358,190	389,253[67]
Bo District	Bo	5,473.6[68]	Southern Province	463,668	527,131[69]
Bonthe District	Mattru Jong	3,468		129,947	137,155[70]
Pujehun District	Pujehun	4,105		228,392	262,073[71]
Moyamba District	Moyamba	6,902		260,910	
Western Area Urban District	Freetown	3,568	Western Area	1,272,873	1,473,873
Western Area Rural District	Waterloo	4,175		174,249	205,400

Economy

Sierra Leone is slowly emerging from a protracted civil war and is showing signs of a successful transition. Investor and consumer confidence continue to rise, adding impetus to the country's economic recovery. There is greater freedom of movement and the successful re-habitation and resettlement of residential areas.

Rich in minerals, Sierra Leone has relied on mining, especially diamonds, for its economic base. The country is among the top 10 diamond producing nations in the world. Mineral exports remain the main foreign currency earner. Sierra Leone is a major producer of gem-quality diamonds. Though rich in diamonds, it has historically struggled to manage their exploitation and export.

Diamond miners in Kono District.

Annual production of Sierra Leone's diamond estimates range between $250–300 million US$. Some of that is smuggled, where it is possibly used for money laundering or financing illicit activities. Formal exports have dramatically improved since the civil war with efforts to improve the management of them having some success. In October 2000, a UN-approved certification system for exporting diamonds from the country was put in place and led to a dramatic increase in legal exports. In 2001, the government created a mining community development fund (DACDF), which returns a portion of diamond export taxes to diamond mining communities. The fund was created to raise local communities' stake in the legal diamond trade.

Sierra Leone is also known for its blood diamonds that were mined and sold to diamond conglomerates during the civil war, in order to buy the weapons that fuelled the atrocities of the civil war.[72] In the 1970s and early 1980s, economic growth rate slowed because of a decline in the mining sector and increasing corruption among government officials.

Percentage of GDP by sector (2007)[73]

Rank	Sector	Percentage of GDP
1	Agriculture	58.5
2	Other Services	10.4
3	Trade and tourism	9.5
4	Wholesale and retail trade	9.0
5	Mining and quarrying	4.5
6	Government Services	4.0
7	Manufacturing and handicrafts	2.0
8	Construction	1.7
9	Electricity and water	0.4

By the 1990s economic activity was declining and economic infrastructure had become seriously degraded. Over the next decade much of the formal economy was destroyed in the country's civil war. Since the end of hostilities in January 2002, massive infusions of outside assistance have helped Sierra Leone begin to recover. Much of the recovery will depend on the success of the government's efforts to limit corruption by officials, which many feel was the chief cause for the civil war. A key indicator of success will be the effectiveness of government management of its diamond sector.

Sierra Leone has one of the world's largest deposits of rutile, a titanium ore used as paint pigment and welding rod coatings. Sierra Rutile Limited, owned by a consortium of United States and European investors, began commercial mining operations near the city of Bonthe, in the Southern Province, in early 1979. It was then the largest non-petroleum US investment in West Africa. The export of 88,000 tons realized $75 million in export earnings in 1990. In 1990, the company and the government made a new agreement on the terms of the company's concession in Sierra Leone. Rutile and bauxite mining operations were suspended when rebels invaded the mining sites in 1995, but exports resumed in 2005. The new Mines and Minerals Act was passed by Parliament in November 2009, which aimed to improve concessions management in the Ministry of Mineral Resources. Sierra Leone is an EITI candidate country.

About two-thirds of the population engages in subsistence agriculture, which accounts for 52.5% of national income. The government is trying to increase food and cash crop production and upgrade small farmer skills. The government works with several foreign donors to operate integrated rural development and agricultural projects.

Despite its successes and development, the Sierra Leone economy still faces significant challenges. There is high unemployment, particularly among the youth and ex-combatants. Authorities have been slow to implement reforms in the civil service, and the pace of the privatisation programme is also slacking and donors have urged its advancement.

Sierra Leone's currency is the Leone. The central bank of the country is the Bank of Sierra Leone which is located in the capital, Freetown. Sierra Leone operates a floating exchange rate system, and foreign currencies can be exchanged at any of the commercial banks, recognised foreign exchange bureaux and most hotels. Credit card use is limited in Sierra Leone, though they may be used at some hotels and restaurants. There are a few internationally linked automated teller machines that accept Visa cards in Freetown operated by ProCredit Bank.

Demographics

Sierra Leone had an estimated 2010 population of 5,245,695 and growth rate of 2.216 percent a year.[8] The country's population is mostly young, with an estimated 41.7 percent under 15, and rural, with an estimated 62 percent of people living outside the cities.[8] As a result of migration to cities the population is becoming more urban with an estimated rate of urbanisation growth of 2.9 percent a year.[8] [74] Population density varies greatly with the country. The Western Area Urban District, including Freetown, the capital and largest city, has a population density of 1,224 persons per square km whereas the largest district Koinadugu has a density of 21.4 persons per square km.[74] Life expectancy in Sierra Leone is 41 years.[75]

A woman in the village of Njama in Kailahun District

Although English is the official language,[76] spoken at schools, government administration and the media, Krio (derived from English and several indigenous African languages), the language to the Sierra Leone Krio people), is the most widely spoken language in virtually all parts of Sierra Leone. The Krio language is spoken by 97% of the country's population[8] [77] and unites all the different ethnic groups, especially in their trade and interaction with each other.[9] In December 2002, Sierra Leone's President Ahmad Tejan Kabbah also named Bengali as an "official language" in recognition of the work of 5,300 troops from Bangladesh in the United Nations Mission in Sierra Leone peacekeeping force.[78] [79]

According to the *World Refugee Survey 2008*, published by the U.S. Committee for Refugees and Immigrants, Sierra Leone had a population of 8,700 refugees and asylum seekers at the end of 2007. Nearly 20,000 Liberian refugees voluntarily returned to Liberia over the course of 2007. Of the refugees remaining in Sierra Leone nearly all were Liberian.[80]

The populations quoted above for the five largest cities are from the 2004 census. Other figures are estimates from the source cited. Different sources give different estimates. Some claim that Magburaka should be included in the above list, but one source estimates the population at only 14,915,[82] whilst another puts it as high as 85,313.[83] "Pandebu-Tokpombu" is presumably the extended town of Torgbonbu which had a population of 10,716 in the 2004 census, though "Gbendembu" had a larger population of 12,139 in that census. In the 2004 census, Waterloo had a population of 34,079.

Religion

Further information: Islam in Sierra Leone and Roman Catholicism in Sierra Leone

Sierra Leone religious sects[84]	
Religion	Percent
Islam	69%
Christianity	30%
African indigenous	1%

Followers of Islam are estimated to comprise 77% of Sierra Leone's population according to the US Department of State,[85] with about 21% followers of Christianity, and 2% of the population practising indigenous animist beliefs. The 2007 UNHCR's "Report on International Religious Freedom in Sierra Leone"[84] estimated 60% Muslim, 20 to 30% Christian and 5 to 10% other beliefs, with many citizens practising a mixture of Islam and traditional indigenous religious beliefs or Christianity and traditional indigenous beliefs. The Pew Research Center estimates the Muslim population at 71.3% (4,059,000).[86] Muslims predominate in all of the country's three provinces and the Western Area, though formerly they were concentrated in the north with the south being mainly Christian. Another estimate puts Christianity in Sierra Leone at 30% of the population, with Islam at 60% and indigenous beliefs at 10%. [87].

The constitution of Sierra Leone provides for freedom of religion and the government generally protects this right and does not tolerate its abuse.

Ethnic groups

Ethnic groups of Sierra Leone [14]
Temne
Mende
Limba
Kono
Mandingo
Krio
Fula
Kuranko
Sherbro
Susu
Loko
Kissi
Yalunka

Vai

Sierra Leone government is home to about sixteen ethnic groups,[88] each with its own language and custom. Unlike most African nations, Sierra Leone has no serious ethnic divisions and no serious religious divisions. People often married across tribal and religious boundaries.

The largest and most dominant groups are the Temne at 35% [14] and the Mende at 31% [14]. The Temne predominate in the Northern Province. The Mende likewise predominate in the South-Eastern Provinces. The Mende, who are believed to be descendants of the Mane, were originally in the Liberian hinterland. They began moving into Sierra Leone slowly and peacefully in the eighteenth century. The Temne are believed to have come from Futa Jallon, which is in present-day Guinea. Sierra Leone's national politics centres on the competition between the north-west, dominated by the Temne, and the south-east dominated by the Mende.

The third-largest ethnic group are the Limba at 8.5% of the population. The Limba are native people of Sierra Leone. They have no tradition of origin and they have always lived in Sierra Leone since it was discovered. The Limba are primarily found in Northern Sierra Leone and they seen as an ally of the Temne. Sierra Leone's first president Siaka Stevens and the country's second president Joseph Saidu Momoh are ethnic Limba.

The fourth largest ethnic group are the Fula at around (8%) of the population (descendants of 17th- and 18th-century Fulani settlers from the Fouta Djalon region of Guinea); they live primarily in the northeast and the western area of Sierra Leone. The Fula are primarily traders and many live in middle class homes. Because of their trading, the Fulas are found in virtually all parts of the country. Some notable ethnic Fula include Sierra Leone's current chief justice Umu Hawa Tejan Jalloh.

The fifth-largest ethnic group are the Mandingo (also known as Mandinka) at 7% (they are the descendants of the Mandinka traders from Guinea, who immigrated to Sierra Leone between 1840 to about 1898). The Mandinka are predominantly found in the east and the northern part of the country, and they are the largest inhabitant of the large towns, most notably Kabal and Falaba in Koinadugu District in the north and Yengema, Kono District in the east of the country. Some notable Mandinka includes Sierra Leone's third president Ahmad Tejan Kabbah, former Sierra Leone's vice president Sorie Ibrahim Koroma and current Sierra Leone natural resources minister Minkailu Mansaray.

After the Mandinka, are the Kono, who live primarily in Kono District in Eastern Sierra Leone. The Kono are descendants from Guinea. The Kono are primarily farmers and diamond miners. Some notable ethnic Kono include current Sierra Leone vice president Alhaji Samuel Sam-Sumana and current Sierra Leone's first lady Sia Nyama Koroma. The Kono are about split between Muslims and Christians.

Behind the Kono, are the Creole (at 5%) (descendants of freed West Indies slaves from the West Indies and freed African American slaves from the United States which landed in Freetown between 1787 and about 1885) are primarily found in the capital city of Freetown and its surrounding Western Area. Creole culture is unlike that of all other ethnic groups in Sierra Leone, and it is typical of Western culture and ideals.

Much smaller ethnic groups are the Kuranko, who are related to the Mandingo. The Kuranko are believed to have begun arriving in Sierra Leone from Guinea in about 1600 and settle in the north. The Loko in the north are native people of Sierra Leone and they have lived in Sierra Leone since it was discovered. The Susu and Yalunka in the far north in Kambia District around the border with Guinea are related people and they are both descendants from Guinea. The Kissi and the much smaller group of Vai, (who are largely Muslim) are further inland in Kailahun District in the East next to the border with Liberia. On the coast in Bonthe District in the south are the Sherbro, who are native people of Sierra Leone and have settled in Sherbro island since it was founded. In the past, Sierra Leoneans were noted for their educational achievements, trading activity, entrepreneurial skills, and arts and crafts work, particularly wood carving. Many are part of larger ethnic networks extending into several countries, which link West African states in the area. But the level of education and infrastructure has declined sharply over the last 30 years.[89]

List of Sierra Leoneans

Education and health

Education in Sierra Leone is legally required for all children for six years at primary level (Class P1-P6) and three years in junior secondary education,[90] but a shortage of schools and teachers has made implementation impossible.[42] Two thirds of the adult population of the country are illiterate.[91] The Sierra Leone Civil War resulted in the destruction of 1,270 primary schools and in 2001 67 percent of all school-age children were out of school.[42] The situation has improved considerably since then with primary school enrolment doubling between 2001 and 2005 and the reconstruction of many schools since the end of the war.[92] Students at primary schools are usually 6 to 12 years old, and in secondary schools 13 to 18. Primary education is free and compulsory in government-sponsored public schools.

A secondary school class in Pendembu

Second grade class in Koidu Town.

The Kailahun Government Hospital at its reopening in 2004.

The country has two universities: Fourah Bay College, founded in 1827 (the oldest university in West Africa),[93] and Njala University, primarily located in Bo District. Njala University was established as the Njala Agricultural Experimental Station in 1910 and became a university in 2005.[94] Teacher training colleges and religious seminaries are found in many parts of the country.

Health care is provided by the government and others. Since April 2010, the government has instituted the Free Health Care Initiative which commits to free services for pregnant and lactating women and children under 5. This policy has been supported by increased aid from the United Kingdom and is recognised as a progressive move that other African countries may follow.[95] The country has a very high infant mortality and a very low life expectancy. The maternal death rates are also the highest in the world, at 2,000 deaths per 100,000 live births. The country suffers from epidemic outbreaks of diseases including yellow fever, cholera, lassa fever and meningitis.[96] The prevalence of HIV/AIDS in the population is 1.6 percent, higher than the world average of 1 percent but lower than the average of 6.1 percent in Sub-Saharan Africa.[97]

Military

The Military of Sierra Leone, officially the Republic of Sierra Leone Armed Forces (RSLAF), are the unified armed forces of Sierra Leone responsible for the territorial security of Sierra Leone's border and defending the national interests of Sierra Leone within the framework of its international obligations. The armed forces were formed after independence in 1961, on the basis of elements of the former British Royal West African Frontier Force present in the country. The Sierra Leone Armed Forces currently consist of around 15,500 personnel, comprising the largest

Sierra Leone Army,[98] the Sierra Leone Navy and the Sierra Leone Air Wing.[99] The president of Sierra Leone is the Commander in Chief of the military, with the Minister of Defence responsible for defence policy and the formulation of the armed forces. The current Sierra Leone Defence Minister is Ret. Major Alfred Paolo Conteh. The Military of Sierra Leone also has a Chief of the Defence Staff who is a uniformed military official responsible for the administration and the operational control of the Sierra Leone military.[100] Brigadier General Alfred Nelson-Williams who was appointed by president Koroma succeeded the retired Major General Edward Sam M'boma on 12 September 2008 as the Chief of Defence Staff of the Military.[101]

Before Sierra Leone gained independence in 1961 the military was known as the Royal Sierra Leone Military Force. The military seized control in 1968, bringing the National Reformation Council into power. On 19 April 1971, when Sierra Leone became a republic, the Royal Sierra Leone Military Forces were renamed the Republic of Sierra Leone Military Force (RSLMF).[102] The RSLMF remained a single service organization until 1979, when the Sierra Leone Navy was established. It then remained largely unchanged for 16 years until in 1995 when Defence Headquarters was established and the Sierra Leone Air Wing formed. This gave the need for the RSLMF to be renamed the Armed Forces of the Republic of Sierra Leone (AFRSL).

Law enforcement

Law enforcement in Sierra Leone is primarily the responsibility of the Sierra Leone Police (SLP). Sierra Leone Police was established by the British colony back in 1894 and is one of the oldest police forces in West Africa. The key mission of the Sierra Leone Police include to prevent crime, to protect life and property, to detect and prosecute offenders, to maintain public order, to ensure safety and security, to enhance access to justice. The Sierra Leone Police is headed by the Inspector General of Police, the professional head of the Sierra Leone Police force and is appointed by the President of Sierra Leone. Each one of Sierra Leone's 14 districts is headed by a District Police commissioner who is the professional head of their respective district. The Districts Police Commissioners report directly to the Inspector General of Police at the Sierra Leone Police headquarters in Freetown. The current Inspector General of Police is Brima Acha Kamara who was appointed to the position by former president Ahmad Tejan Kabbah.

Transportation

There are a number of systems of transport in Sierra Leone, which has a road, air and water infrastructure, including a network of highways and several airports. There are 11,300 kilometres[103] of highways in Sierra Leone, of which 904 km (562 mi)[103] are paved (about 8% of the roads). Sierra Leone highways are linked to Conakry, Guinea, and Monrovia, Liberia. Sierra Leone has the largest natural harbour on the African continent, allowing international shipping through the Queen Elizabeth II Quay in the Cline Town area of eastern Freetown or through Government Wharf in central Freetown. There are 800 km (497 mi) of waterways in Sierra Leone, of which 600 km (373 mi) are navigable year-round. Major port cities are Bonthe, Freetown, Sherbro Island and Pepel.

The road from Kenema to Kailahun District.

There are ten regional airports in Sierra Leone, and one international airport. The Lungi International Airport located in the coastal town of Lungi in Northern Sierra Leone is the primary airport for domestic and international travel to or from Sierra Leone. Passengers cross the river to Aberdeen Heliports in Freetown by hovercraft, ferry or a helicopter. Helicopters are also available from the airport to other major cities in the country. The airport has paved runways longer than 3,047m. The other airports have unpaved runways, and seven have runways 914 to 1,523 metres long; the remaining two have shorter runways. This country appears on the E.U. list of prohibited countries with regard to the certification of airlines. This means that no airline which is Sierra Leone registered may operate services of any kind within the European Union. This is due to substandard safety standards.[104]

Drinking water supply

Water supply in Sierra Leone is characterized by limited access to safe drinking water. Despite efforts by the government and numerous non-governmental organizations, access has not much improved since the end of the Sierra Leone Civil War in 2002, stagnating at about 50% and even declining in rural areas.[105] In the capital Freetown, taps often run dry. It is hoped that a new dam in Orugu, for which China committed financing in 2009, will alleviate water scarcity.[106]

According to a national survey (Multiple Indicator Cluster Survey) carried out in 2006, 84% of the urban population and 32% of the rural population had access to an improved water source. Those with access in rural areas were served almost exclusively by protected wells. The 68% of the rural population without access to an improved water source relied on surface water (50%), unprotected wells (9%) and unprotected springs (9%). Only 20% of the urban population and 1% of the rural population had access to piped drinking water in their home. Compared to the 2000 survey access has increased in urban areas, but has declined in rural areas, possibly because facilities have broken down because of a lack of maintenance.[105] [107]

With a new decentralization policy, embodied in the Local Government Act of 2004, responsibility for water supply in areas outside the capital was passed from the central government to local councils. In Freetown the Guma Valley Water Company remains in charge of water supply.

Culture

The arts

The arts in Sierra Leone are a mixture of tradition and hybrid African and western styles.[108] [109] [110]

Sports

Football is by far the most popular sport in Sierra Leone. The national football team, popularly known as the Leone Stars, represents the country in international competitions. It has never qualified for the FIFA World Cup but participated in the 1994 and 1996 African Cup of Nations. The country's national television network, The Sierra Leone Broadcasting Service (SLBS) broadcasts the live match, along with several radio stations throughout the country. Some well known Sierra Leonean footballers include the team captain Mohamed Kallon, Julius Gibrilla Woobay, Al Bangura, Paul Kpaka, Rodney Strasser, Ahmed Deen, Samuel Barlay, Kewullay Conteh ex Stevenage player Denzil Conteh, Albert Jarrett and Kei Kamara

The Sierra Leone National Premier League is the top football league, controlled by the Sierra Leone Football Association. The two biggest and most successful football clubs are East End Lions and Mighty Blackpool, but Kallon F.C. has enjoyed contemporary success. Kallon F.C. won the Premier League and the Sierra Leonean FA Cup in 2006,

Sierra Leonean football star Sheriff Suma just after a Leone Stars training session on 4 Sept. 2008 at the National Stadium in Freetown.

and eliminated 2006 Nigerian Premier League Champions Ocean Boys FC in the 2007 CAF Champions League first qualifying round, but later lost to ASEC Mimosas of Ivory Coast in the second qualifying round for the group stage.

The Sierra Leone U-17 football team, nicknamed the Sierra Stars, finished as runner-up at the 2003 African U-17 Championship in Swaziland, but came in last place in their group at the 2003 FIFA U-17 World Championship in Finland.

The Sierra Leone cricket team represents Sierra Leone in international cricket competitions, and is among the best in West Africa. It became an affiliate member of the International Cricket Council in 2002. It made its international debut at the 2004 African Affiliates Championship, where it finished last of eight teams. But at the equivalent tournament in 2006, Division Three of the African region of the World Cricket League, it finished as runner-up to Mozambique, and just missed a promotion to Division Two.

In 2009 the Sierra Leone Under-19 team finished second in the African Under-19 Championship in Zambia, thus qualifying for the Under-19 World Cup qualifying tournament with nine other teams.[111] However, the team was unable to obtain Canadian visas to play in the tournament, which was held in Toronto.[112]

The Sierra Leone national basketball team represents Sierra Leone in international men's basketball competitions and is controlled by the Sierra Leone Basketball Federation. The squad is mostly home-based, with a few foreign players.

Media

Media in Sierra Leone began with the introduction of the first printing press in Africa at the start of the nineteenth century. A strong journalistic tradition developed with the creation of a number of newspapers. In the 1860s, the country became a journalist hub for Africa, with professionals travelling to the country from across the continent. At the end of the nineteenth century, the industry went into decline, and when radio was introduced in the 1930s, it became the primary communication media in the country. The Sierra Leone Broadcasting Service (SLBS) was created by the government in 1934 making it the earliest English language radio broadcaster service in West Africa. The service began broadcasting television in 1963, with coverage extended to all the districts in the country in 1978.

Radio listener in Kailahun

Print media is not widely read in Sierra Leone, especially outside Freetown, partially due to the low levels of literacy in the country.[113] In 2007 there were 15 daily newspapers in the country, as well as those published weekly.[114] Among newspaper readership, young people are likely to read newspapers weekly and older people daily. The majority of newspapers are privately run and are often critical of the government. The standard of print journalism tends to be low due to lack of training, and people trust the information published in newspapers less than that found on the radio.[113]

Isata Mahoi shown editing radio programmes in Talking Drum studio Freetown, she is also an actress in Sierra Leone radio soap opera Atunda Ayenda

Radio is the most-popular and most-trusted media in Sierra Leone, with 85% of people having access to a radio and 72% of people in the country listening to the radio daily.[113] These levels do vary between areas of the country, with the Western Area having the highest levels and Kailahun the lowest. Stations mainly consist of local commercial stations with a limited broadcast range, combined with a few stations with national coverage. The United Nations Mission in Sierra Leone (UNIOSIL) runs one of the most popular stations in the country, broadcasting programs in a range of languages. Content includes news of UN activities and human rights information, as well as music and news. The UN missions will withdraw in 2008 and the UN Radio's future is uncertain. There is also a government station run by the SLBS that transmits on FM and short-wave. FM relays of BBC World Service, Radio France Internationale and Voice of America are also broadcast.

Outside the capital Freetown television is not watched by a great many people. There are two national, free terrestrial television stations in Sierra Leone, one run by the government SLBS and the other a private station, ABC Television-Africa (ABC). In 2007, a pay-per-view service was also introduced by GTV as part of a pan-African television service in addition to the nine year old sub-Saharan Digital satellite television service (DStv) originating from Multichoice Africa in South Africa. Internet access in Sierra Leone has been sparse but is on the increase, especially since the introduction of wireless services across the country. There are nine internet service providers (ISPs) operating in the country. Freetown has a city wide wireless network and internet cafes and other businesses offering internet access. Problems experienced with access to the Internet include an intermittent electricity supply and a slow connection speed in the country outside Freetown.

The Sierra Leone constitution guarantees freedom of speech, and freedom of the press; however, the government maintains strong control of media, and at times restricts these rights in practice. Some subjects are seen as taboo by society and members of the political elite; imprisonment and violence have been used by the political establishment against journalists.[115] [116] Under legislation enacted in 1980, all newspapers must register with the Ministry of Information and pay sizeable registration fees. The Criminal Libel Law, including Seditious Libel Law of 1965, is used to control what is published in the media.[116] In 2006, President Ahmad Tejan Kabbah committed to reforming the laws governing the press and media to create a freer system for journalists to work in,[116] but in 2007, Sierra Leone was ranked as having the 121st least-free press in the world, with the press less-free, in comparison to other countries, than in 2006.[117]

See also

Additional, more specific, and related topics may be found at:

- Alexander Falconbridge
- Commonwealth of Nations
- Paul Cuffee
- Stephen Rapp

Notes

[1] ""Country Profile:Sierra Leone"" (http://www.fco.gov.uk/en/travel-and-living-abroad/travel-advice-by-country/country-profile/sub-saharan-africa/sierra-leone). . Retrieved 2011-09-19.

[2] ""Rebuild Sierra-leone"" (http://live.rebuildsierraleone.org/index.php?/about-sierra-leone.htm). . Retrieved 2011-09-19.

[3] "Sierra Leone" (http://www.imf.org/external/pubs/ft/weo/2010/01/weodata/weorept.aspx?sy=2007&ey=2010&scsm=1&ssd=1&sort=country&ds=.&br=1&c=724&s=NGDPD,NGDPDPC,PPPGDP,PPPPC,LP&grp=0&a=&pr.x=81&pr.y=10). International Monetary Fund. . Retrieved 21 April 2010.

[4] Encarta Encyclopedia. "Sierra Leone" (http://encarta.msn.com/encyclopedia_761563681/Sierra_Leone.html). *Sierra Leone*. . Retrieved 19 February 2008.

[5] FCO.gov.uk (http://www.fco.gov.uk/en/travel-and-living-abroad/travel-advice-by-country/country-profile/sub-saharan-africa/sierra-leone)

[6] The World Guide. "Sierra Leone Geography" (http://sbs.com.au/theworldnews/Worldguide/index.php3?country=178&header=3). . Retrieved 19 February 2008.

[7] http://www.indexmundi.com/sierra_leone/population_below_poverty_line.html

[8] "Sierra Leone" (https://www.cia.gov/library/publications/the-world-factbook/geos/sl.html). *The World Factbook*. CIA. . Retrieved 21 June 2009.

[9] Eprints.soas.ac.uk (https://eprints.soas.ac.uk/181/)

[10] http://allafrica.com/stories/200409290746.html

[11] http://www.sierraleonedailymail.com/archives/822

[12] http://arabnews.com/world/article373733.ece?service=print

[13] http://www.care.org/newsroom/specialreports/sierra_leone/sl_relief.asp

[14] http://www.state.gov/r/pa/ei/bgn/5475.htm

[15] Kup (1961), p. 116

[16] Classic Encyclopedia. "Sierra Leone" (http://www.1911encyclopedia.org/Sierra_Leone). . Retrieved 19 February 2008.

[17] Room (1995), p. 346-7

[18] Kingfisher Geography encyclopedia. ISBN 1-85613-582-9. Page 180

[19] History World. "History of Sierra Leone" (http://www.historyworld.net/wrldhis/PlainTextHistories.asp?historyid=ad45). . Retrieved 19 February 2008.

[20] Countries and Their Cultures. "Culture of Sierra Leone" (http://www.everyculture.com/Sa-Th/Sierra-Leone.html). . Retrieved 22 February 2008.

[21] Encyclopaedia Britannica. "Sierra Leone History" (http://www.britannica.com/eb/article-55344/Sierra-Leone). . Retrieved 19 February 2008.

[22] Encyclopedia of the Nations. "Sierra Leone - History" (http://www.nationsencyclopedia.com/Africa/Sierra-Leone-HISTORY.html). . Retrieved 22 February 2008.

[23] Utting (1931), p. 33

[24] Utting (1931), p. 8

[25] LeVert, Suzanne (2006). *Cultures of the World: Sierra Leone*. Marshall Cavendish (published 2007). p. 22. ISBN 9780761423348

[26] Sibthorpe, A. B. C. (1970). *The History of Sierra Leone*. Routledge. p. 7. ISBN 9780714617695

[27] National Maritime Museum. "Sir John Hawkins" (http://www.nmm.ac.uk/collections/explore/object.cfm?ID=BHC2755). . Retrieved 9 December 2008.

[28] Pham (2005). *Child soldiers, adult interests: the global dimensions of the Sierra Leonean tragedy* (http://books.google.com/?id=ZnPFKpwoIkIC&pg=PA32&dq=sierra+leone+independence+1961#v=onepage&q=sierra leone independence 1961&f=false). Nova Publishers. pp. 4–8. ISBN 9781594546716. .

[29] "Sierra Leone's struggle for progress" (http://www.economist.com/world/mideast-africa/displaystory.cfm?story_id=12775514). *The Economist*. 11 December 2008. . Retrieved 22 August 2010.

[30] Harris, Sheldon H. *Paul Cuffe: Black America and the African Return* (New York: Simon and Schuster, 1972) pp. 32-33, and especially note 15 on p. 140

[31] Sierra-leone.org (http://www.sierra-leone.org/heroes5.html). Retrieved on 17 January 2007].

[32] Martin Killson, *Political Change in a West African State: A Study of the Modernization Process in Sierra Leone*, Cambridge, Massachusetts, USA, 1966, p 60. Also pp 106, 107, 110, 111, 186-188 on other riots and strikes.

[33] Advocate Nations of Africa: Sierra Leone (http://www.advocatenations.org/html/sierra_leone.html)

[34] "Sierra Leone's Leader; Milton Augustus Strieby Margai, New York Times, April 28, 1961" (http://select.nytimes.com/gst/abstract.html?res=F30816FE3B5912738DDDA10A94DC405B818AF1D3&scp=1&sq=milton+margai&st=p). Select.nytimes.com. 28 April 1961. . Retrieved 22 August 2010.

[35] Pham, John-Peter (2005). *Child soldiers, adult interests: the global dimensions of the Sierra Leonean tragedy* (http://books.google.com/?id=ZnPFKpwoIkIC&pg=PA32&dq=sierra+leone+independence+1961#v=onepage&q=sierra leone independence 1961&f=false). Nova Publishers. pp. 32–33. ISBN 9781594546716. .

[36] McKenna, Amy (2011). *The History of Western Africa* (http://books.google.com/?id=uuRvYdibcGYC&pg=PA206&dq=history+of+sierra+leone+civil+war#v=onepage&q=history of sierra leone civil war&f=false). he Rosen Publishing Group. pp. 202–203. ISBN 9781615303991. .

[37] Pham, John-Peter (2005). *Child soldiers, adult interests: the global dimensions of the Sierra Leonean tragedy* (http://books.google.com/?id=ZnPFKpwoIkIC&pg=PA32&dq=sierra+leone+independence+1961#v=onepage&q=sierra leone independence 1961&f=false). Nova Publishers. pp. 33–35. ISBN 9781594546716. .

[38] "Sierra Leone: End of the Exception" (http://www.time.com/time/magazine/article/0,9171,941075,00.html?iid=chix-sphere). *Time* (USA). 31 March 1967. . Retrieved 24 February 2011.

[39] Gberie, Lansana (2005). *A dirty war in West Africa: the RUF and the destruction of Sierra Leone* (http://books.google.com/?id=OeBYQAFPXxsC&pg=PA34&dq=sierra+leone+independence+1961#v=onepage&q=independence 1961&f=false). C. Hurst & Co. Publishers. pp. 26–27. ISBN 9781850657422. .

[40] Besada, Hany (2009). *From civil strife to peace building: examining private sector involvement in West African reconstruction* (http://books.google.com/?id=pr8qPdm64akC&pg=PA103&dq=history+sierra+leone+"Siaka+Stevens"#v=onepage&q=history sierra leone "Siaka Stevens"&f=false). Wilfrid Laurier Univ. Press. pp. 103–105. ISBN 9781554580521. .

[41] Rotberg, Robert I. (2003). *State failure and state weakness in a time of terror* (http://books.google.com/?id=oajfCpTpgCIC&pg=PA80&dq=sierra+leone+"1973+election"#v=onepage&q=sierra leone "1973 election"&f=false). Brookings Institution Press. pp. 80. ISBN 9780815775744. .

[42] "Sierra Leone" (http://www.dol.gov/ilab/media/reports/iclp/tda2001/Sierra-leone.htm). *2001 Findings on the Worst Forms of Child Labor*. Bureau of International Labor Affairs, U.S. Department of Labor (2002).

[43] Gberie, Lansana (2005). *A dirty war in West Africa: the RUF and the destruction of Sierra Leone* (http://books.google.com/?id=OeBYQAFPXxsC&pg=PA34&dq=sierra+leone+independence+1961#v=onepage&q=independence 1961&f=false). C. Hurst & Co. Publishers. pp. 5–6. ISBN 9781850657422. .

[44] Bah, M. (1998). *The Worlds Most Resilient People*. London: Alpha.

[45] LeVert, Suzanne (2006). *Cultures of the World: Sierra Leone*. Marshall Cavendish (published 2007). p. 7. ISBN 9780761423348

[46] Blinker, Linda (September 2006). *Country Environment Profile (CEP) Sierra Leone* (http://www.delsle.ec.europa.eu/en/whatsnew/Docs/Final Report Country Environmental Profile (CEP) SL 19-OCT-06.pdf). Freetown, Sierra Leone: Consortium Parsons Brinckerhoff. p. 12. . Retrieved 25 September 2008

[47] LeVert, Suzanne (2006). *Cultures of the World: Sierra Leone*. Marshall Cavendish (published 2007). pp. 8–9. ISBN 9780761423348

[48] C. Michael Hogan. 2009. *Painted Hunting Dog: Lycaon pictus*, GlobalTwitcher.com, ed. N. Stromberg (http://globaltwitcher.auderis.se/artspec_information.asp?thingid=35993)

[49] Rhett Butler. 2005. *Sierra Leone: Environmental Profile*, mongabay.com (http://rainforests.mongabay.com/20sierraleone.htm)

[50] Environmental Justice Foundation "Sierra Leone" (http://www.ejfoundation.org/page370.html), 17 September 2009

[51] BBC News, *Sierra Leone sets up forest park* (http://news.bbc.co.uk/2/hi/africa/7136606.stm), 10 December 2007

[52] Nyulawglobal.org (http://www.nyulawglobal.org/globalex/Sierra_Leone.htm)

[53] "Country profile: Sierra Leone" (http://news.bbc.co.uk/2/hi/africa/country_profiles/1061561.stm). BBC News. 18 June 2008. . Retrieved 5 August 2008.

[54] News.sl (http://news.sl/drwebsite/publish/article_20057492.shtml)

[55] *Background Note: Sierra Leone* (http://www.state.gov/r/pa/ei/bgn/5475.htm). U.S. Department of State. October 2008. . Retrieved 7 October 2008

[56] *Welcome to the Mano River Union Website* (http://www.manoriverunion.org/). Mano River Union. 2006. . Retrieved 7 October 2008

[57] *Ministry of Foreign Affairs and International Relations* (http://www.daco-sl.org/encyclopedia/1_gov/1_2mfa.htm). Sierra Leone Encyclopedia. 2007. . Retrieved 7 October 2008

[58] http://www.ssrnetwork.net/documents/Publications/SierraLeoneWPs/working%20paper%209.pdf

[59] Renner-Thomas, Ade (2010). *Land Tenure in Sierra Leone: The Law, Dualism and the Making of a Land Policy* (http://books.google.com/?id=RiIpW6vWVPoC&pg=PA5&dq="population+of+Sierra+Leone"#v=onepage&q="population of Sierra Leone"&f=false). AuthorHouse. pp. 6–7. ISBN 9781449058661. .

[60] "ActionAid launches Perception survey as new local councils struggle to survive" (http://www.actionaid.org/tanzania/index.aspx?PageID=3925). ActionAid. . Retrieved 26 February 2011.

[61] "Final Results 2004 population and housing census" (http://www.daco-sl.org/encyclopedia/1_gov/1_4/Statistics Sierra Leone/ssl_final_results.pdf) (PDF). Statistics Sierra Leone. p. 3. . Retrieved 9 June 2008.

[62] World Gazetteer: Bombali - profile of geographical entity including name variants (http://www.world-gazeteer.com/wg.php?x=&men=gpro&lng=en&des=wg&srt=npan&col=adhoq&msz=1500&geo=-6636) at www.world-gazetteer.com

[63] World-gazetteer.com (http://www.world-gazetteer.com/wg.php?x=&men=gpro&lng=en&des=wg&srt=npan&col=adhoq&msz=1500&geo=-6644)

[64] World Gazetteer: Tonkolili - profile of geographical entity including name variants (http://www.world-gazetteer.com/wg.php?x=&men=gpro&lng=en&des=wg&srt=npan&col=adhoq&msz=1500&geo=-6647) at www.world-gazetteer.com

[65] World Gazetteer: Kambia - profile of geographical entity including name variants (http://www.world-gazetteer.com/wg.php?x=&men=gpro&lng=en&des=wg&srt=npan&col=adhoq&msz=1500&geo=-6639) at www.world-gazetteer.com

[66] World Gazetteer: Kenema - profile of geographical entity including name variants (http://www.world-gazetteer.com/wg.php?x=& men=gpro&lng=en&des=wg&srt=npan&col=adhoq&msz=1500&geo=-6640) at www.world-gazetteer.com

[67] World Gazetteer: Kailahun - profile of geographical entity including name variants (http://www.world-gazetteer.com/wg.php?x=& men=gpro&lng=en&des=wg&srt=npan&col=adhoq&msz=1500&geo=-6638) at www.world-gazetteer.com

[68] "Bo District" (http://www.daco-sl.org/encyclopedia/3_dist/3_1a_bo.htm). Sierra Leone Encyclopedia (UN and Government of Sierra Leone). July 2007. . Retrieved 6 June 2008.

[69] World Gazetteer: Bo - profile of geographical entity including name variants (http://www.world-gazetteer.com/wg.php?x=& men=gpro&lng=en&des=wg&srt=npan&col=adhoq&msz=1500&geo=-6635) at www.world-gazetteer.com

[70] World-gazetteer.com (http://www.world-gazetteer.com/wg.php?x=&men=gpro&lng=en&des=wg&srt=npan&col=adhoq& msz=1500&geo=-6637)

[71] World Gazetteer: Pujehun - profile of geographical entity including name variants (http://www.world-gazetteer.com/wg.php?x=& men=gpro&lng=en&des=wg&srt=npan&col=adhoq&msz=1500&geo=-6645) at www.world-gazetteer.com

[72] "UN targets 'blood diamonds' trade" (http://news.bbc.co.uk/1/hi/world/africa/3117421.stm). *BBC News*. 1 August 2003. . Retrieved 28 April 2011.

[73] African Development Bank, OECD - Organisation for Economic Co-operation and Development (2009). *African Economic Outlook 2009: Country Notes: Volumes 1 and 2* (http://books.google.com/?id=e91T-0zSWnAC&pg=PT565&dq=mining+gdp+sierra+ leone#v=onepage&q=mining gdp sierra leone&f=false). OECD Publishing. pp. 562. ISBN 9789264076181. .

[74] Renner-Thomas, Ade (2010). *Land Tenure in Sierra Leone: The Law, Dualism and the Making of a Land Policy* (http://books.google. com/?id=RiIpW6vWVPoC&pg=PA5&dq="population+of+Sierra+Leone"#v=onepage&q="population of Sierra Leone"&f=false). AuthorHouse. p. 5. ISBN 9781449058661. .

[75] MacKenzie, Julia (4 January 2007). "Sierra Leone's failing health" (http://news.bbc.co.uk/2/hi/programmes/newsnight/6231905.stm). *BBC News*. . Retrieved 7 April 2010.

[76] "Sierra Leone Overview" (http://www.sl.undp.org/sloverview.htm). United Nations Development Programme Sierra Leone. . Retrieved 3 June 2008.

[77] Krio Translation Services (http://www.language9.com/languages/translation/krio-translation.html)

[78] "Sierra Leone makes Bengali official language" (http://www.dailytimes.com.pk/default.asp?page=story_29-12-2002_pg9_6). . Retrieved 29 December 2002.

[79] Zahurul Alam (27 December 2002). "Bangla Made One of The Official Languages of Sierra Leone" (http://www.voanews.com/bangla/ archive/2002-12/a-2002-12-27-3-Bangla.cfm?mod). .

[80] "World Refugee Survey 2008" (http://www.refugees.org/survey). U.S. Committee for Refugees and Immigrants. 19 June 2008. .

[81] "Sierra Leone: largest cities and towns and statistics of their population" (http://world-gazetteer.com/wg.php?x=1273962075& men=gcis&lng=en&des=wg&geo=-195&srt=2pnn&col=abcdefghinoq&msz=1500&pt=c&va=&srt=p2nn). World Gazetteer. 2010. . Retrieved 26 February 2011.

[82] "Population Of Magburaka" (http://population-of.com/en/Sierra-Leone/02/Magburaka). Population-of.com. . Retrieved 22 August 2010.

[83] "Exaf" (http://www.exaf.eu/exaf/page.php?pid=210). Exaf.eu. . Retrieved 22 August 2010.

[84] UNHCR.org (http://www.unhcr.org/refworld/docid/4cf2d06b43.html)

[85] US Department of State estimate (http://www.state.gov/g/drl/rls/irf/2007/90119.htm)

[86] Pewforum.org (http://pewforum.org/uploadedfiles/Topics/Demographics/Muslimpopulation.pdf)

[87] http://www.containersofhope.com/sierra-leone.html

[88] *About Sierra Leone* (http://www.daco-sl.org/encyclopedia/1_gov/1_1gosl.htm). Sierra Leone Encyclopedia. 2007. . Retrieved 27 July 2008

[89] "Sierra Leone (02/08)" (http://www.state.gov/r/pa/ei/bgn/5475.htm). *"U.S. Department of State"*. . Retrieved 17 February 2008.

[90] Wang, Lianqin (2007). *Education in Sierra Leone: Present Challenges, Future Opportunities*. World Bank Publications. p. 2. ISBN 0821368680

[91] "Human Development Report 2009 - Proportion of international migrant stocks residing in countries with very high levels of human development (%)" (http://hdrstats.undp.org/en/indicators/20.html). Hdrstats.undp.org. . Retrieved 22 August 2010.

[92] Wang, Lianqin (2007). *Education in Sierra Leone: Present Challenges, Future Opportunities*. World Bank Publications. p. 1 and 3. ISBN 0821368680

[93] *Commonwealth Education Partnerships 2007* (http://books.google.com/?id=ID5XqeV4q10C&pg=PT326&dq=sierra+leone+"Fourah+ Bay+College"+"west+africa"+oldest&cd=12#v=onepage&q=sierra leone "Fourah Bay College" "west africa" oldest). Nexus Strategic Partnerships Ltd. 2006. ISBN 0954962915. .

[94] *Njala University College (Nuc)* (http://www.daco-sl.org/encyclopedia/1_gov/1_7njala.htm). Sierra Leone: Sierra Leone Encyclopedia. July. . Retrieved 25 June 2008

[95] "Sierra Leone" (http://www.kambia.org.uk/information_about/sierra_leone.htm). The Kambia Appeal. . Retrieved 24 January 2008.

[96] "The Primary Health Care Hand Book Policing" (http://www.health.sl/drwebsite/publish/healthcare.shtml) (doc). Ministry of Health & Sanitation. 25 May 2007. . Retrieved 24 January 2008.

[97] "2006 Report on the global AIDS epidemic" (http://www.unaids.org/en/KnowledgeCentre/HIVData/GlobalReport/Default.asp) (PDF). UNAIDS. 2006. . Retrieved 24 January 2008.

[98] Armed forces (Sierra Leone) Jane's Sentinel Security Assessments (http://www.janes.com/extracts/extract/wafrsu/siers100.html), June 2008

[99] "Summary (Sierra Leone) - Jane's World Air Forces" (http://www.janes.com/articles/Janes-World-Air-Forces/Summary-Sierra-Leone. html). Janes.com. 30 July 2010. . Retrieved 22 August 2010.

[100] News.sl (http://www.news.sl/drwebsite/publish/article_200511647.shtml)

[101] New Vision, Freetown, 15 September 2008

[102] Partners: Sierra Leone Armed Forces (http://www.daco-sl.org/encyclopedia/1_gov/1_6rslaf.htm)

[103] CIA - The World Factbook (https://www.cia.gov/library/publications/the-world-factbook/geos/sl.html)

[104] List of banned E.U. air carriers (http://ec.europa.eu/transport/air-ban/pdf/list_en.pdf)

[105] WHO / UNICEF Joint Monitoring Programme for Water Supply and Sanitation: Estimates for the use of Improved Drinking-Water Sources (http://www.wssinfo.org/fileadmin/user_upload/resources/SLE_wat.pdf), Sierra Leone, updated March 2010

[106] OOSKA News: China Lends $28.8 Million USD to Sierra Leone for Orugu Dam (http://www.ooskanews.com/middle-east-africa/ china-lends-288-million-usd-sierra-leone-orugu-dam), 15 June 2009

[107] Nataliya Pushak; Vivien Foster (June 2011). "Sierra Leone's Infrastructure. A Continental Perspective" (http://www-wds.worldbank.org/ external/default/WDSContentServer/WDSP/IB/2011/06/29/000158349_20110629104032/Rendered/PDF/WPS5713.pdf). Policy Research Working Paper 571. World Bank. pp. 31–35. . Retrieved 6 August 2011.

[108] Banham, Martin (2004). A history of theatre in Africa (http://books.google.com/?id=RZXtk9bCZ-8C&pg=PA171&dq=theatre+of+ sierra+leone#v=onepage&q=theatre of sierra leone&f=false). Cambridge University Press. p. 171. ISBN 9780521808132. .

[109] Conteh, Prince Sorie (2009). Traditionalists, Muslims, and Christians in Africa: interreligious encounters and dialogue (http://books. google.com/?id=HpAuyiMRTDcC&pg=PA23&dq=visual+art+sierra+leone#v=onepage&q=visual art sierra leone&f=false). Cambria Press. pp. 23–24. ISBN 9781604975963. .

[110] Manson, Katrina; James Knight (2009). Sierra Leone (http://books.google.com/?id=VxRcEzkFs-wC&pg=PA43&dq=music+of+ sierra+leone#v=onepage&q=music of sierra leone&f=false). Bradt Travel Guides. pp. 42–45. ISBN 9781841622224. .

[111] Cricinfo article Uganda and Sierra Leone Win Through (http://www.cricinfo.com/other/content/story/403002.html)

[112] Cricinfo article: Visa Issues End Sierra Leone's World Cup Dream (http://www.cricinfo.com/other/content/story/423890.html)

[113] Media use, and attitudes towards media in Sierra Leone:A comprehensive baseline study (http://downloads.bbc.co.uk/worldservice/ trust/pdf/media_report_2007.pdf). BBC World Service Trust and Search for Common Ground. June 2007. . Retrieved 19 April 2007

[114] Jalloh, Tanu (28 December 2007). Sierra Leone: Newspaper Development (http://allafrica.com/stories/200712310637.html). Freetown, Sierra Leone: Concord Times. . Retrieved 19 April 2008

[115] Wilson, Harry (2005). Press Freedoms and Human Rights:2005 Year End Press Freedom Brief (http://web.archive.org/web/ 20071124131843/http://www.cpu.org.uk/pf_2005_review.html). Commonwealth Press Union. Archived from the original (http://www. cpu.org.uk/pf_2005_review.html) on 24 November 2007. . Retrieved 20 April 2008

[116] Sierra Leone - Annual report 2006 (http://www.rsf.org/article.php3?id_article=17400). Reporters without Borders:For Press Freedom. 2006. . Retrieved 20 April 2008

[117] Worldwide Press Freedom Index 2007 (http://www.rsf.org/article.php3?id_article=24025). Reporters without Borders:For Press Freedom. 2007. . Retrieved 20 April 2008

Book references

Primary sources

• Keen, David (2005). Conflict and Collusion in Sierra Leone (http://books.google.com/?id=SEz1PCvILHUC& printsec=frontcover&dq=Conflict+&+Collusion+in+Sierra+Leone). Oxford: James Currey. ISBN 0-85255-883-X. ISBN 9780852558836.

• Kup, Alexander Peter (1961). A History of Sierra Leone, 1400-1787. Cambridge: Cambridge University Press. ISBN 0786418141.

• Sillinger, Brett (2003). Sierra Leone: Current Issues and Background. New York: Nova Science Publishers. ISBN 1590336623.

• Utting, Francis A (1931). The Story of Sierra Leone. Ayer Company Publishers. ISBN 0836967046.

• Beah, Ishmael. A Long Way Gone: Memoirs of a Boy Soldier (2007). Sarah Crichton Books: New York. Link: A Long Way Gone

Secondary sources

- Room, Adrian (1995). *Placenames of the World*. Jefferson, NC: McFarland. ISBN 0786418141.
- Levinson, Robby (1998). *Ethnic Groups Worldwide: A Ready Reference Handbook*. Phoenix: Oryx Press. ISBN 1573560197.

Further reading

- Abraham, Arthur (1978). *Mende Government and Politics under Colonial Rule*. Freetown and London.
- Abraham, Arthur (1978). *Cultural Policy in Sierra Leone*. UNESCO.
- Abraham, Arthur (1978). "Sengbe Pieh: A Neglected Hero?". *Journal of the Historical Society of Sierra Leone* **II** (2).
- Abraham, Arthur (c. 1976). *Topics in Sierra Leone History: A Counter-Colonial Interpretation*. Sierra Leone: Leone Publishers.
- Awoonor-Gordon, John (2001). *The Worlds Most Resilient People*. London.
- Bah, M. Alpha (1998). *Fulbe Migration in Sierra Leone: A Case History of Twentieth-Century Migration and Settlement Among the Kissi of Koindu*. New York: Peter Lang Publishing.
- Berger, Daniel (2003). *In the Land of Magic Soldiers: A Story of White and Black in West Africa*. Farrar, Straus and Giroux.
- Blyden, Nemata Amelia. *'In Her Majesty' Service: West Indians in British Colonial Government, Sierra Leone, 1808-1880: Race, Class and Ethnicity in a British West African Colony*.
- Clarke, J.I., Nelson, S.J.A. and Swindell, K. (1966). *Sierra Leone in Maps*. London.
- Cole, Bernadette (1995). *Mass Media, Freedom and Democracy in Sierra Leone*. Freetown.
- Conteh-Morgan, Earl and Dixon-Fyle, Mac (1999). *Sierra Leone at the End of the Twentieth Century: History, Politics and Society*. New York: Peter Lang Publishing.
- Cox-George, N. A. (1961). *Finance and Development in West Africa: The Sierra Leone Experience*. London: D. Dobson.
- Foray, Cyril P. (1977). *Historical Dictionary of Sierra Leone*. Metuchen and London: The Scarecrow Press.
- Forna, Aminatta (2002). *The Devil that danced on the Water: A daughter's memoir*. London.
- Fyfe, Christopher (1962). *A History of Sierra Leone*. Cambridge University Press, Oxford University Press.
- Fyle, Christopher (1964). *Sierra Leone Inheritance*. London.
- Fyfe, Christopher (1992). *Africanus Horton, 1835-1883 : West African Scientist and Patriot*. Aldershot.
- Gberie, Lansana, Smillie, Ian and Hazleton, Ralph (January 2000). *The Heart of the Matter: Sierra Leone, Diamonds and Human Society*. Partnership Africa Canada.
- Global Witness (June 2000). *Conflict Diamonds, Possibilities for the Identification, Certification and Control of Diamonds*.
- Hirsch; John L. (2000). *Sierra Leone: Diamonds and the Struggle for Democracy*. Lynne Rienner Pub.
- Jalloh, Alusine (1999). "African Entrepreneurship: Muslim Fula Merchants in Sierra Leone". *Monographs in International Studies, Africa Series* (Ohio University Center for International Studies) (71).
- Jalloh, S. Balimo (1991). *Sierra Leone*. Länderbericht, Bergisch Gladbach.
- Jalloh, S. Balimo (February 2001). "Conflicts, Resources and Social Instability in Subsahara Africa – The Sierra Leone Case". *Internationasles Afrikaforum* (37): 166–180.
- Jalloh, S. Balimo (April 1995). "Subsahara Africa – Trade Expansion Through Countertrade". *Internationales Afrikaforum*: 365–374.
- Jones, Durosimi Eldred (1965). *Othellos Countrymen*. Oxford University Press.
- Jones, Durosimi Eldred and Eustace Palmer (1995). *African Literature Today Africa World Press*. London.
- Jones, Howard (1986). *Mutiny on the Amistad: The Saga of a Slave Revolt and its Impact on American Abolition, Law and Diplomacy*. New York: Oxford University Press.

- Kabba, Muctaru, (Editor) (1988). *Sierra Leonean Heroes, Fifty Great Men and Women Who Helped to Build Our Nation*. Freetown.
- Koroma, Abdul K. (1996). *Sierra Leone – The Agony of a Nation*. Freetown: Andromeda Publications.
- Kpundeh, Sahr John. *Politics and Corruption in Africa: A Case Study of Sierra Leone*. Lanham: University Press of America.
- Lewis, Damien (2005). *Operation Certain Death - The Inside Story of the SAS'S Greatest Battle*. Arrow Books.
- Nicol, Davidson, *Regionalism and the New International Economic Order*; UNITAR-CEESTEM-Club of Rome conference at the United Nations, Pergamon Press, 1981.
- Opala, Joseph (1987). *The Gullah: Rice, Slavery, and the Sierra Leone-American Connection*. U.S. Information Service.
- William Reno (1995). *Corruption and State Politics in Sierra Leone*. Cambridge University Press.
- Paul Richards (1996). *Fighting for the Rain Forest – War Youth & Resources in Sierra Leone*. London: James Currey Publishers.
- Sawyerr, Harry (1970). *God, Ancestor or Creator? Aspects of Traditional Belief in Ghana, Nigeria & Sierra Leone*. Harlow: Longmans.
- H.L. van der Laan (1965). *The Sierra Leone Diamonds, An Economic Study covering the years 1952-1961*. Oxford.
- Wyse, Akintola J.G.; Deveneaux, Gustav H.K. (1993). *The Sierra Leone-German connection, 1787-1987, An Overview*. Freetown: The German Embassy.
- Wyse, Akintola J. G. (1990). *H. C. Bankole-Bright and Politics in Colonial Sierra Leone, 1919-1958*. Cambridge, New York: Cambridge University Press.
- Mwakikagile, Godfrey (2001). *The Modern African State: Quest for Transformation*, Chapter Two: Anarchy and Mercenaries in Sierra Leone: The Powerless African State, pp. 19 – 72. Nova Science Publishers, Inc., Huntington, New York; Mwakikagile, Godfrey, *Military Coups in West Africa Since The Sixties*, Chapter Twelve: Sierra Leone, pp. 183 – 196, Nova Science Publishers, 2001.

External links

Government

- The Republic of Sierra Leone (http://www.statehouse.gov.sl/) official government site
- Chief of State and Cabinet Members (https://www.cia.gov/library/publications/world-leaders-1/world-leaders-s/sierra-leone.html)
- Ministry of Mineral Resources (http://www.slminerals.org/) official government minerals site

General information

- Country Profile (http://news.bbc.co.uk/1/hi/world/africa/country_profiles/1061561.stm) from BBC News
- Sierra Leone (https://www.cia.gov/library/publications/the-world-factbook/geos/sl.html) entry at *The World Factbook*
- Sierra Leone (http://ucblibraries.colorado.edu/govpubs/for/sierraleone.htm) from *UCB Libraries GovPubs*
- Sierra Leone (http://www.dmoz.org/Regional/Africa/Sierra_Leone/) at the Open Directory Project
- Wikimedia Atlas of Sierra Leone
- Development Assistance Coordination Office: *Sierra Leone Encyclopedia 2008* (http://www.daco-sl.org/encyclopedia/)

News media

- Awareness Times (http://news.sl/) Newspaper
- The New People (http://www.thenewpeople.com) The New People Newspaper
- Sierra Eye (http://www.sierraeye.net) Sierra Leone News Portal
- News headline links (http://allafrica.com/sierraleone/) from AllAfrica.com

- Sierra Leone News & Blog (http://www.my-sierra-leone-life.com) Current Sierra Leone News & Blog
- Sierra Leone world (http://www.edoworld.net/sierra_Leone_world_Home.html) News headline, information and analysis

Tourism

- National Tourist Board of Sierra Leone (http://www.sierraleonetourism.sl/) official site
- Sierra Leone travel guide from Wikitravel

Telecommunication

- Sierra Leone (http://www.alosmart.com/Sierra-Leone-calling-card-191.asp) telecom

Other

- Friends of Sierra Leone (http://fosalone.org)
- Masanga (http://www.masanga.co.uk) Grace's Fund for Masanga Hospital
- Schools for Salone (http://www.schoolsforsalone.org) non-profit dedicated to rebuilding schools
- ENCISS (http://www.enciss-sl.org/) civil society and governance
- Aisha's Eye on Sierra Leone (http://www.lawrence.edu/dept/religious_studies/aysesierraleone/home.html) a photo documentary
- The Auradicals Club (http://auradicals.com/) Student Club in Fourah Bay College
- Sierra Leone Web (http://www.sierra-leone.org)
- Sweet Salone (http://www.sweetsalone.com) 2008 film on new music in Sierra Leone
- War Crimes Trials in Sierra Leone (http://www.sc-sl.org)
- Sierra Leone Photo Gallery (http://photo.lacina.net/country-22-sierra-leone.html)
- Hurrarc - Human Rights Respect Awareness Raising Campaigners - Sierra Leone Ngo (http://www.hurrarc.org)
- Environmental Justice Foundation's report on pirate fishing in Sierra Leone (http://www.ejfoundation.org/page370.html)

bjn:Sierra Leone mrj:Сьерра-Леоне

Guinea

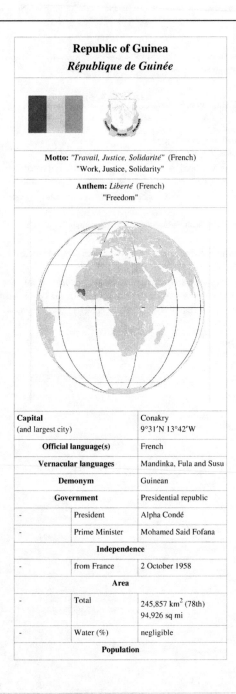

Republic of Guinea	
République de Guinée	

Motto: *"Travail, Justice, Solidarité"* (French)
"Work, Justice, Solidarity"

Anthem: *Liberté* (French)
"Freedom"

Capital (and largest city)	Conakry 9°31′N 13°42′W
Official language(s)	French
Vernacular languages	Mandinka, Fula and Susu
Demonym	Guinean
Government	Presidential republic
- President	Alpha Condé
- Prime Minister	Mohamed Said Fofana
Independence	
- from France	2 October 1958
Area	
- Total	245,857 km² (78th) 94,926 sq mi
- Water (%)	negligible
Population	

-	July 2009 estimate	10,057,975[1] (81st)
-	1996 census	7,156,407
-	Density	40.9/km^2 106.1/sq mi
GDP (PPP)		2010 estimate
-	Total	$10.807 billion[2]
-	Per capita	$1,046[2]
GDP (nominal)		2010 estimate
-	Total	$4.633 billion[2]
-	Per capita	$448[2]
Gini (1994)		40.3 (medium)
HDI (2010)		0.340 (low) (156th)
Currency		Guinean franc (GNF)
Time zone		(UTC+0)
Drives on the		right
ISO 3166 code		GN
Internet TLD		.gn
Calling code		224

Guinea /ˈgɪni/, officially the **Republic of Guinea** (French: *République de Guinée*), is a country in West Africa. Formerly known as French Guinea (*Guinée française*), it is today sometimes called **Guinea-Conakry** to distinguish it from its neighbour Guinea-Bissau.[3] Guinea is divided into eight administrative regions and subdivided into thirty-three prefectures. Conakry is the capital, largest city and economic center. The other major cities in the country include Labe, Nzérékoré, Kankan, Kindia, Mamou, Boke, and Guéckédou.

Guinea's 10 million people belong to twenty-four ethnic groups. The largest and most prominent groups are the Fula 43% (French: *Peul*; Fula: *Fulɓe*), Mandinka 35%, and Susu 20%

Guinea has almost 246000 square kilometres (94981 sq mi). It forms a crescent by curving from its western border on the Atlantic Ocean toward the east and the south. Its northern border is shared with Guinea-Bissau, Senegal, and Mali, the southern one with Sierra Leone, Liberia, and Côte d'Ivoire. The Niger River arises in Guinea and runs eastward.

History

The land that is now Guinea belonged to a series of African empires until France colonized it in the 1890s, and made it part of French West Africa.[4] Guinea declared its independence from France on 2 October 1958.[4] Since independence, Guinea has had autocratic rule in which one person possesses unlimited power, which has contributed to making Guinea one of the poorest countries in the world.[5] [6] [7]

Monument to commemorate the 1970 military victory over the Portuguese invasion

Governments since independence

Ahmed Sékou Touré became President upon Guinea's independence. By violent oppression, he ruled until 26 March 1984, when he died unexpectedly.[8] [9] By a quick coup d'état, Lansana Conté became the President after Touré. By despotic means, Conté clung to power until his death in 2008. Despite extraordinary aluminium rich resources, he was unable to improve the desperate economic plight into which Touré had plunged the country.[10]

On 23 December 2008, Moussa Dadis Camara seized control of Guinea as the head of a junta.[11] On 28 September 2009, the junta ordered its soldiers to attack people who had gathered to protest any attempt by Camara to become President.[12] The soldiers went on a rampage of rape, mutilation, and murder.[13]

On 3 December 2009, an aide shot Camara during a dispute about the rampage of September 2009. Camara went to Morocco for medical care.[13] [14] Vice-President (and defense minister) Sékouba Konaté flew back from Lebanon to run the country in Camara's absence.[15]

On 12 January 2010 Camara was flown from Morocco to Burkina Faso.[16] After meeting in Ouagadougou on 13 and 14 January, Camara, Konaté and Blaise Compaoré, President of Burkina Faso, produced a formal statement of twelve principles promising a return of Guinea to civilian rule within six months. It was agreed that the military would not contest the forthcoming elections, and Camara would continue his convalescence outside Guinea.[17] On 21 January 2010 the military junta appointed Jean-Marie Doré as Prime Minister of a six-month transition government, leading up to elections.[18]

The presidential election was set to take place on 27 June and 18 July 2010,[19] [20] it was held as being the first free and fair election since independence in 1958. The first round took place normally on the 27 June 2010 with ex Prime Minister Cellou Dalein Diallo and his rival Alpha Condé emerging as the two runners-up for the second round.[21] However, due to allegations of electoral fraud, the second round of the election was postponed until 19 September 2010.[22] A delay until 10 October was announced by the electoral commission (CENI), subject to approval by Sekouba Konaté.[23] Yet another delay until 24 October was announced in early October.[24] Elections were finally held on 7 November. Voter turnout was high, and the elections went relatively smoothly.[25]

16 November 2010, Alpha Condé, the leader of the opposition party Rally of the Guinean People (RGP), was officially declared the winner of a 7 November run-off in Guinea's presidential election. He has promised to reform the security sector and review mining contracts if elected.[26]

On the night of July 18, 2011, President Conde's residence was attacked in an attempted coup. The attack included a fierce firefight and rocket propelled grenades. The president was unharmed.[27] Sixteen people have been charged with the attempted assassination. Most of those indicted are close associates of Sekouba Konaté.[28]

The legal voting age is 18.

Regions and prefectures

The Republic of Guinea covers 245857 square kilometres (94926 sq mi) of West Africa about 10 degrees north of the equator. Guinea is divided into four natural regions with distinct human, geographic, and climatic characteristics:

- Maritime Guinea (*La Guinée Maritime*) covers 18% of the country
- Mid-Guinea (*La Moyenne-Guinée*) covers 20% of the country
- Upper-Guinea (*La Haute-Guinée*) covers 38% of the country
- Forested Guinea (*Guinée forestière*) covers 23% of the country, and is both forested and mountainous

Guinea is divided into seven administrative regions and subdivided into thirty-three prefectures.

Regions of Guinea

Satellite image of Guinea

Region	Capital	Population(2010)
Conakry Region	Conakry	2,325,190
Nzérékoré Region	Nzérékoré	1,528,908
Kankan Region	Kankan	1,427,568
Kindia Region	Kindia	1,326,727
Boké Region	Boké	965,767
Labé Region	Labé	903,386
Faranah Region	Faranah	839,083
Mamou Region	Mamou	719,011

- The capital Conakry with a population of 1,548,470 ranks as a special zone.

Geography

At 245 800 km^2 (310 sq mi), Guinea is roughly the size of the United Kingdom and slightly smaller than the US state of Oregon. There are 300 km (190 mi) of coastline and a total land border of 3400 km (2100 mi). Its neighbours are Côte d'Ivoire (Ivory Coast), Guinea-Bissau, Liberia, Mali, Senegal and Sierra Leone. It lies mostly between latitudes 7° and 13°N, and longitudes 7° and 15°W (a small area is west of 15°).

The country is divided into four main regions: the Basse-Coté lowlands, populated mainly by the Susu ethnic group; the cooler, mountainous Fouta Djallon that run roughly north-south through the middle of the country, populated by Fulas, the Sahelian Haute-Guinea to the northeast, populated by Malinké, and the forested jungle regions in the southeast, with several ethnic groups. Guinea's mountains are the source for the Niger, the Gambia, and Senegal Rivers, as well as the numerous rivers flowing to the sea on the west side of the range in Sierra Leone and Ivory Coast.

Map of Guinea

The highest point in Guinea is Mount Nimba at 1750 m (5740 ft). Although the Guinean and Ivorian sides of the Nimba Massif are a UNESCO Strict Nature Reserve, the portion of the so-called Guinean Backbone continues into Liberia, where it has been mined for decades; the damage is quite evident in the Nzérékoré Region at 7°32'17"N 8°29'50"W.

Economy

Guinea has abundant natural resources including 25% or more of the world's known bauxite reserves. Guinea also has diamonds, gold, and other metals. The country has great potential for hydroelectric power. Bauxite and alumina are currently the only major exports. Other industries include processing plants for beer, juices, soft drinks and tobacco. Agriculture employs 80% of the nation's labor force. Under French rule, and at the beginning of independence, Guinea was a major exporter of bananas, pineapples, coffee, peanuts, and palm oil.

Mining

Richly endowed with minerals, Guinea possesses over 25 billion tonnes (metric tons) of bauxite — and perhaps up to one-half of the world's reserves. In addition, Guinea's mineral wealth includes more than 4-billion tonnes of high-grade iron ore, significant diamond and gold deposits, and undetermined quantities of uranium. Guinea has considerable potential for growth in agricultural and fishing sectors. Soil, water, and climatic conditions provide opportunities for large-scale irrigated farming and agro industry. Possibilities for investment and commercial activities exist in all these areas, but Guinea's poorly developed infrastructure and rampant corruption continue to present obstacles to large-scale investment projects.

Joint venture bauxite mining and alumina operations in northwest Guinea historically provide about 80% of Guinea's foreign exchange. Bauxite is refined into alumina, which is later smelted into aluminium. The *Compagnie des Bauxites de Guinea* (CBG), which exports about 14 million tonnes of high-grade bauxite annually, is the main player in the bauxite industry. CBG is a joint venture, 49% owned by the Guinean Government and 51% by an international consortium known as Halco Mining Inc., a joint venture of Dadco Mining and Rio Tinto Alcan.[29] The *Compagnie des Bauxites de Kindia* (CBK), a joint venture between the Government of Guinea and Russki Alumina, produces some 2.5 million tonnes annually, nearly all of which is exported to Russia and Eastern Europe. Dian Dian, a Guinean/Ukrainian joint bauxite venture, has a projected production rate of 1000000 t (short tons; long tons) per year, but is not expected to begin operations for several years. The *Alumina Compagnie de Guinée* (ACG), which took over the former Friguia Consortium, produced about 2.4 million tonnes in 2004 as raw material for its alumina refinery. The refinery exports about 750,000 tonnes of alumina. Both Global Alumina and Alcoa-Alcan have signed conventions with the Government of Guinea to build large alumina refineries with a combined capacity of about 4 million tonnes per year.

Diamonds and gold also are mined and exported on a large scale. AREDOR, a joint diamond-mining venture between the Guinean Government (50%) and an Australian, British, and Swiss consortium, began production in 1984 and mined diamonds that are 90% gem quality. Production stopped from 1993 until 1996, when First City Mining, of Canada, purchased the international portion of the consortium. The bulk of diamonds are mined artisanally. The largest gold mining operation in Guinea is a joint venture between the government and Ashanti Goldfields of Ghana. Société Minière de Dinguiraye (SMD) also has a large gold mining facility in Lero, near the Malian border.

Guinea has large reserves of the steel-making raw material, iron ore. Rio Tinto is the majority owner of the $6 billion Simandou iron ore project, which the firm says is the world's best unexploited resource.[30] Rio Tinto has signed a binding agreement with Aluminum Corp. of China Ltd. to establish the joint venture for the Simandou iron ore project. This project is said to be of the same magnitude as the Pilbara in Western Australia . In the 1960s, Thomas Price, then vice president of US-based steel company Kaiser Steel, said, "I think this [the Pilbara] is one of the most massive ore bodies in the world."[31]

Problems and reforms

The Guinean Government adopted policies in the 1990s to return commercial activity to the private sector, promote investment, reduce the role of the state in the economy, and improve the administrative and judicial framework. Guinea has the potential to develop, if the government carries out its announced policy reforms, and if the private sector responds appropriately. So far, corruption and favouritism, lack of long-term political stability, and the lack of a transparent budgeting process continue to dampen foreign investor interest in major projects in Guinea.

Reforms since 1985 include eliminating restrictions on agriculture and foreign trade, liquidation of some government-owned corporations, the creation of a realistic exchange rate, increased spending on education, and cutting the government bureaucracy. In July 1996, President Lansana Conté appointed a new government, which promised major economic reforms, including financial and judicial reform, rationalization of public expenditures, and improved government revenue collection. Under 1996 and 1998 International Monetary Fund (IMF)/World Bank agreements, Guinea continued fiscal reforms and privatization, and shifted governmental expenditures and internal reforms to the education, health, infrastructure, banking, and justice sectors.

The government revised the private investment code in 1998 to stimulate economic activity in the spirit of free enterprise. The code does not discriminate between foreigners and nationals and allows for repatriation of profits. While the code restricts development of Guinea's hydraulic resources to projects in which Guineans have majority shareholdings and management control, it does contain a clause permitting negotiations of more favourable conditions for investors in specific agreements. Foreign investments outside Conakry are entitled to more favourable terms. A national investment commission has been formed to review all investment proposals. Guinea and the United States have an investment guarantee agreement that offers political risk insurance to American investors through the Overseas Private Investment Corporation (OPIC). In addition, Guinea has inaugurated an arbitration court system, which allows for the quick resolution of commercial disputes.

Cabinet changes in 1999, which increased corruption, economic mismanagement, and excessive government spending, combined to slow the momentum for economic reform. The informal sector continues to be a major contributor to the economy.

Until June 2001, private operators managed the production, distribution, and fee-collection operations of water and electricity under performance-based contracts with the Government of Guinea. However, the two utilities are plagued by inefficiency and corruption. Foreign private investors in these operations departed the country in frustration.

In 2002, the IMF suspended Guinea's Poverty Reduction and Growth Facility (PRGF) because the government failed to meet key performance criteria. In reviews of the PRGF, the World Bank noted that Guinea had met its spending goals in targeted social priority sectors. However, spending in other areas, primarily defense, contributed to a significant fiscal deficit. The loss of IMF funds forced the government to finance its debts through Central Bank advances. The pursuit of unsound economic policies has resulted in imbalances that are proving hard to correct.

Under then-Prime Minister Diallo, the government began a rigorous reform agenda in December 2004 designed to return Guinea to a PRGF with the IMF. Exchange rates have been allowed to float, price controls on gasoline have been loosened, and government spending has been reduced while tax collection has been improved. These reforms have not reduced inflation, which hit 27% in 2004 and 30% in 2005. Currency depreciation is also a concern. The Guinea franc was trading at 2550 to the dollar in January 2005. It hit 5554 to the dollar by October 2006.

Despite the opening in 2005 of a new road connecting Guinea and Mali, most major roadways remain in poor repair, slowing the delivery of goods to local markets. Electricity and water shortages are frequent and sustained, and many businesses are forced to use expensive power generators and fuel to stay open.

Even though there are many problems plaguing Guinea's economy, not all foreign investors are reluctant to come to Guinea. Global Alumina's proposed alumina refinery has a price tag above $2 billion. Alcoa and Alcan are proposing a slightly smaller refinery worth about $1.5 billion. Taken together, they represent the largest private investment in sub-Saharan Africa since the Chad-Cameroon oil pipeline. Also, Hyperdynamics Corporation, an American oil company, signed an agreement in 2006 to develop Guinea's offshore Senegal Basin oil deposits in a concession of 31000 square miles (80000 km^2); it is pursuing seismic exploration.[32]

On 13 October 2009, Guinean Mines Minister Mahmoud Thiam announced that the Chinese International Fund would invest more than $7bn (£4.5bn) in infrastructure. In return, he said the firm would be a "strategic partner" in all mining projects in the mineral-rich nation. He said the firm would help build ports, railway lines, power plants, low-cost housing and even a new administrative centre in the capital, Conakry. However, analysts say that the timing of the deal is likely to stir controversy, as the legitimacy of Guinea's government is under question.[33]

Youth unemployment, however, remains a large problem. Guinea needs an adequate policy to address the concerns of the urban youth. The problem is the disparity between their life and what they see on television. As the youth cannot find jobs, seeing the economic power and consumerism of richer countries only serves to frustrate them further.[34]

Oil

Northwest Africa's coast has now been assessed and is ready for oil development, and Guinea is actively being courted in this endeavor. Guinea signed a Production sharing agreement with Hyperdynamics Corporation (Houston, TX) in 2006 to explore a large offshore tract, recently in partnership with Dana Petroleum PLC (Aberdeen, United Kingdom). The initial well, the Sabu-1, is scheduled to begin drilling in October 2011 at a site in approximately 700 meters of water. The Sabu-1 will target a four-way anticline prospect with upper Cretaceous sands and is anticipated to be drilled to a total depth of 3,600 meters.[35]

Transportation

Further information: Rail transport in Guinea

The railway which operated from Conakry to Kankan ceased operating in the mid-1980s . Domestic air services are intermittent. Most vehicles in Guinea are 20+ years old, and cabs are any four-door vehicle which the owner has designated as being for hire. Locals, nearly entirely without vehicles of their own, rely upon these taxis (which charge per seat) and small buses to take them around town and across the country. There is some river traffic on the Niger and Milo rivers. Horses and donkeys pull carts, primarily to transport construction materials.

Iron mining at Simandou (South) in the southeast beginning in 2007 and at Kalia in the east is likely to result in the construction of a new heavy-duty standard gauge railway and deepwater port. Iron mining at Simandou North will load to a new port near Buchanan in Liberia, in exchange for which, rehabilitation of the Conakry to Kankan line will occur.

Conakry International Airport is the largest airport in the country, with flights to other cities in Africa as well as to Europe.

Demography

The population of Guinea is estimated at 10.2 million. Conakry, the capital and largest city, is the hub of Guinea's economy, commerce, education, and culture.

Languages

The official language of Guinea is French. Other significant languages spoken are Maninka (Malinke), Susu, Pular (Fulfulde or Fulani), Kissi, Kpelle, and Loma.

It is also quite common that the people of Guinea also like to use their **feet for sign language**. They do this through series of dances and also

Guinean children

by sitting on the ground and using their feet more effectively. This is mostly seen in the Western area.

Ethnicity

The population of Guinea comprises about 24 ethnic groups. The Fulas or Fulani (French: *Peuls*; Fula: *Fulbe*), comprise 43% of the population and are mostly found in the Futa djallon region. The Mandinka, also known as Mandingo or Malinké, comprise 35% of the population and are mostly found in eastern Guinea concentrated around the Kankan and Kissidougou prefectures. The Soussou, comprising 20%, are predominantly in western areas around the capital Conakry, Forécariah, and Kindia. Smaller ethnic groups make up the remaining 15% of the population, including Kpelle, Kissi, Zialo, Toma and others. The Mandinka, Soussou or(Jallonke, Kpelle, Kissi, Zialo, Toma, Jahanke all speak Mande branch of Niger-Congo language family. Thus this group combined together constitute majority of the population. Non-Africans total about 10,000 (mostly Lebanese, French, and other Europeans).[36]

Religion

Further information: Islam in Guinea

Islam is the majority religion. Approximately 85% of the population is Muslim, while 8% is Christian, and 7% holds traditional animist beliefs. Guinean Muslims are generally Sunni and Sufi;[37] there are relatively few Shi'a in Guinea. Christian groups include Roman Catholics, Anglicans, Baptists, Seventh-day Adventists, and other Evangelical groups. Jehovah's Witnesses are active in the country and recognized by the Government. There is a small Baha'i community. There are small numbers of Hindus, Buddhists, and traditional Chinese religious groups among the expatriate community.[38]

Military

The Conakry Grand Mosque in Guinea, one of the largest mosques in West Africa

Guinea's armed forces are divided into five branches – army, navy, air force, the paramilitary National Gendarmerie and the Republican Guard – whose chiefs report to the Chairman of the Joint Chiefs of Staff, who is subordinate to the Minister of Defense. In addition, regime security forces include the National Police Force (Sûreté National). The Gendarmerie, responsible for internal security, has a strength of several thousand.

The army, with about 15,000 personnel, is by far the largest branch of the armed forces. It is mainly responsible for protecting the state borders, the security of administered territories, and defending Guinea's national interests. Air force personnel total about 700. The force's equipment includes several Russian-supplied fighter planes and transports. The navy has about 900 personnel and operates several small patrol craft and barges.

Healthcare

Guinea has been reorganizing its health system since the Bamako Initiative of 1987 formally promoted community-based methods of increasing accessibility of drugs and health care services to the population, in part by implementing user fees.[39] The new strategy dramatically increased accessibility through community-based healthcare (including community ownership and local budgeting), resulting in more efficient and equitable provision of services. A comprehensive strategy was extended to all areas of health care, with subsequent improvement in health indicators and improvement in health care efficiency and cost.[40] Guinea's public health code is defined by Law No. L/97/021/AN of 19 June 1997 promulgating the Public Health Code. The law provides for the protection and promotion of health and for the rights and duties of the individual, the family, and community throughout the territory of the Republic of Guinea.[41]

In June 2011, the Guinean government announced the establishment of an air solidarity levy on all flights taking off from national soil, with funds going to UNITAID to support expanded access to treatment for HIV/AIDS, TB and malaria.[42] Guinea is among the growing number of countries and development partners using market-based transactions taxes and other innovative financing mechanisms to expand financing options for health care in resource-limited settings.

Maternal and Child Health Care

In June 2011, the United Nations Population Fund released a report on The State of the World's Midwifery [29]. It contained new data on the midwifery workforce and policies relating to newborn and maternal mortality for 58 countries. The 2010 maternal mortality rate per 100,000 births for Guinea is 680. This is compared with 859.9 in 2008 and 964.7 in 1990. The under 5 mortality rate, per 1,000 births is 146 and the neonatal mortality as a percentage of under 5's mortality is 29. The aim of this report is to highlight ways in which the Millennium Development Goals can be achieved, particularly Goal 4 – Reduce child mortality and Goal 5 – improve maternal death. In Guinea the number of midwives per 1,000 live births is 1 and 1 in 26 shows us the lifetime risk of death for pregnant women. [43]

HIV/AIDS

The first cases of HIV/AIDS were reported in 1986. Though levels of AIDS are significantly lower than in a number of other African countries, as of 2005, Guinea was considered by the World Health Organization to face a generalized epidemic.

An estimated 170,000 adults and children were infected at the end of 2004. The spread of the epidemic was attributed to factors such as proximity to high-prevalence countries, a large refugee population, internal displacement and subregional instability.[44] [45]

Culture

Like other West African countries, Guinea has a rich musical tradition. The group Bembeya Jazz became popular in the 1960s after Guinean independence.

Education

The literacy rate of Guinea is one of the lowest in the world: in 2003 it was estimated that only 29.5% of adults were literate (42.6% of males and 18.1% of females).[46] Primary education is compulsory for 8 years, but most children do not attend for so long, and many do not go to school at all. In 1999, primary school attendance was 40 percent.Children, particularly girls, are kept out of school in order to assist their parents with domestic work or agriculture.[47]

See also

Additional, more specific, and related topics may be found at:

• List of Guineans

Schoolgirls in Conakry, Guinea

References

[1] Central Intelligence Agency (2009). "Guinea" (https://www.cia.gov/library/publications/the-world-factbook/geos/gv.html). The World Factbook. . Retrieved 28 January 2010.

[2] "Guinea" (http://www.imf.org/external/pubs/ft/weo/2011/01/weodata/weorept.aspx?sy=2008&ey=2011&scsm=1&ssd=1& sort=country&ds=.&br=1&c=656&s=NGDPD,NGDPDPC,PPPGDP,PPPPC,LP&grp=0&a=&pr.x=79&pr.y=3). International Monetary Fund. . Retrieved 21 April 2011.

[3] See, for example, Univ. of Iowa map (http://www.uiowa.edu/~africart/toc/countries/Guinea-Conakry.html), Music Videos of Guinea Conakry – Clips Guineens (http://www.musicvideos.the-real-africa.com/guinea/), The Anglican Diocese of Guinea – Conakry (http:// netministries.org/see/churches/ch00472), Canal France International's English-language page for Guinea Conakry (http://www.cfi.fr/ partenaires_en.php3?id_rubrique=24&id_article=473)

[4] "History of Guinea" (http://www.historyofnations.net/africa/guinea.html). Historyofnations.net. . Retrieved 28 March 2010.

[5] Zounmenou, David (2 January 2009). "Guinea: Hopes for Reform Dashed Again" (http://allafrica.com/stories/200901020524.html). allAfrica.com. . Retrieved 27 December 2009.

[6] "UN Human Development Report 2009" (http://hdrstats.undp.org/en/countries/country_fact_sheets/cty_fs_GIN.html). Hdrstats.undp.org. . Retrieved 28 March 2010.

[7] Ross, Will (2 October 2008). "Africa | Guineans mark '50 years of poverty'" (http://news.bbc.co.uk/2/hi/africa/7647962.stm). BBC News. . Retrieved 28 March 2010.

[8] Suleiman, Rashid (6 October 2008). "African Dictators – Ahmed Sékou Touré: The 'Father of Coups'" (http://www.politicalarticles.net/ blog/2008/10/06/african-dictators-ahmed-sekou-toure-the-father-of-coups/). PoliticalArticles.Net. . Retrieved 23 December 2009.

[9] Walker, Peter (23 December 2008). "Q&A: Guinea" (http://www.guardian.co.uk/world/2008/dec/23/ guinea-ahmed-sekou-conte-lansana-toure). The Guardian (London). . Retrieved 23 December 2009.

[10] McGreal, Chris (23 December 2008). "Lansana Conté profile: Death of an African 'Big Man'" (http://www.guardian.co.uk/world/2008/ dec/23/lansana-conte-profile). The Guardian (London). . Retrieved 23 December 2009.

[11] Walker, Peter (23 December 2008). "Army steps in after Guinea president Lansana Conté dies" (http://www.guardian.co.uk/world/2008/ dec/23/guinea-dictator-lansana-conte-dies). The Guardian (London). . Retrieved 23 December 2009.

[12] "Guinea massacre toll put at 157" (http://news.bbc.co.uk/2/hi/8280603.stm). London: BBC. 29 September 2009. . Retrieved 23 December 2009.

[13] MacFarquhar, Neil (21 December 2009). "U.N. Panel Calls for Court in Guinea Massacre" (http://www.nytimes.com/2009/12/22/ world/africa/22guinea.html). The New York Times. . Retrieved 23 December 2009.

[14] "Guinean soldiers look for ruler's dangerous rival" (http://www.malaysianews.net/story/573838). malaysianews.net. 5 December 2009. . Retrieved 23 December 2009.

[15] Guinea's presidential guard explains assassination motive (http://news.xinhuanet.com/english/2009-12/16/content_12658142.htm). Xinhua. 16 December 2009.

[16] Brahima Ouedraogo, "Guinea leader arrives in Burkina Faso", Associated Press/Yahoo News (12 Jan 2009) (http://news.yahoo.com/s/ ap/20100112/ap_on_re_af/af_burkina_faso_guinea_leader)

[17] celine says:. ""In Full: Declaration Made in Burkina Faso Between Dadis Camara and Sekouba Konate", Newstime Africa (January 16, 2010)" (http://www.newstimeafrica.com/archives/10414). Newstimeafrica.com. . Retrieved 28 March 2010.

[18] "Guinea junta officially names Dore prime minister" (http://www.reuters.com/article/idUSLDE60K1L120100121?type=marketsNews). Reuters, 21 January 2010.

[19] afrol News – Election date for Guinea proposed (http://www.afrol.com/articles/35415). Afrol.com. Retrieved on 28 June 2011.

[20] Guinea to hold presidential elections in six months _English_Xinhua (http://news.xinhuanet.com/english/2010-01/16/ content_12820272.htm). News.xinhuanet.com (16 January 2010). Retrieved on 28 June 2011.

[21] "Guinea election goes to run-off as Diallo falls short" (http://www.bbc.co.uk/news/10499343). BBC News. 3 July 2010. .

[22] "Guinea sets date for presidential run-off vote" (http://www.bbc.co.uk/news/world-africa-10920366). BBC News. 9 August 2010. .

[23] Saliou Samb, "Guinea election body proposes 10 October run-off", "Reuters" (Sept 20 2010) (http://www.reuters.com/article/ idUSTRE68L5RX20100922). Reuters.com. Retrieved on 28 June 2011.

[24] "Guinea run-off election date set", "Al Jazeera" (5 Oct 2010) (http://english.aljazeera.net/news/africa/2010/10/201010521331725239. html). English.aljazeera.net (5 October 2010). Retrieved on 28 June 2011.

[25] "Guinea sees big turnout in presidential run-off poll", "BBC" (7 Nov 2010) (http://www.bbc.co.uk/news/world-africa-11705147). Bbc.co.uk (7 November 2010). Retrieved on 28 June 2011.

[26] Conde declared victorious in Guinea – Africa | IOL News (http://www.iol.co.za/news/africa/conde-declared-victorious-in-guinea-1. 831341). IOL.co.za (16 November 2010). Retrieved on 28 June 2011.

[27] http://allafrica.com/stories/201107190453.html.

[28] http://allafrica.com/stories/201108050223.html

[29] Saliou Samb, Richard Valdmanis, David Clarke and Jason Neely, "Glitch halts Guinea's CBG bauxite exports-sources - Update 1", Reuters (14 Sept 2011) (http://www.reuters.com/article/2011/09/14/guinea-cbg-exports-idUSL5E7KE3EY20110914)

[30] Saliou Samb and Daniel Magnowski, "One dead in Guinea protest, mine trains stop", Reuters (1 November 2008) (http://www. minesandcommunities.org/article.php?a=8889)

[31] Stephen Pincock, "Iron Ore Country", *ABC Science* (14 July 2010) (http://www.abc.net.au/science/articles/2010/07/14/2953402.htm)

[32] "Joint Venture Opportunity Offshore the West Coast of Africa" (http://www.hyperdynamics.com/media/ HDY-JV-Partner-Opportunity-Brochure-082208.pdf). .Hyperdynamics Corporation (2008)

[33] "Guinea confirms huge China deal" (http://news.bbc.co.uk/1/hi/world/africa/8304418.stm). London: BBC News. 13 October 2009. . Retrieved 13 October 2009.

[34] Joschka Philipps, "Explosive youth: Focus", D+C (Development and Cooperation), funded by Germany's Federal Ministry for Economic Cooperation and Development, (2010/05) pages 190-193 (http://www.inwent.org/ez/articles/171240/index.en.shtml)

[35] * *Hyperdynamics News Releases* (http://investors.hyperdynamics.com/releasedetail.cfm?ReleaseID=600343)

[36] Guinea (08/09) (http://www.state.gov/r/pa/ei/bgn/2824.htm). U.S. Department of State.

[37] Kenneth Harrow, "A Sufi Interpretation of 'Le Regard du Roi'", *Research in African Literature* v. 14 no. 2 (Summer, 1983) (http://www. jstor.org/pss/3818383)

[38] International Religious Freedom Report 2008: Guinea (http://www.state.gov/g/drl/rls/irf/2008/108372.htm). United States Bureau of Democracy, Human Rights and Labor (29 December 2008). *This article incorporates text from this source, which is in the public domain.*

[39] "User fees for health: a background" (http://web.archive.org/web/20061128203803/http://www.eldis.org/healthsystems/userfees/ background.htm). Archived from the original (http://www.eldis.org/healthsystems/userfees/background.htm) on 28 November 2006. . Retrieved 28 December 2006.

[40] "Implementation of the Bamako Initiative: strategies in Benin and Guinea" (http://www.ncbi.nlm.nih.gov/entrez/query. fcgi?cmd=Retrieve&db=PubMed&list_uids=10173105&dopt=Abstract). . Retrieved 28 December 2006.

[41] "WHO – International Digest Of Health Legislation – Guinea – IA. Constitutional provisions relating to health, general health codes or public health laws, human rights, and other fundamental provisions" (http://www.who.int/idhl-rils/results.cfm?language=english& type=ByCountry&strRefCode=Guin&strTopicCode=IA). World Health Organisation. . Retrieved 30 September 2007.

[42] UNITAID. *Republic of Guinea Introduces Air Solidarity Levy to Fight AIDS, TB and Malaria.* (http://www.unitaid.eu/en/resources/ news/347-republic-of-guinea-introduces-air-solidarity-levy-to-fight-aids-tb-and-malaria.html) Accessed 5 July 2011.

[43] "The State Of The World's Midwifery" (http://www.unfpa.org/sowmy/report/home.html). United Nations Population Fund. Accessed August 2011. .

[44] "Status of HIV/AIDS in Guinea, 2005" (http://www.who.int/hiv/HIVCP_GIN.pdf) (PDF). World Health Organisation. 2005. . Retrieved 30 September 2007.

[45] "Epidemiological Fact Sheets: HIV/AIDS and Sexually Transmitted Infections, December 2006" (http://www.who.int/GlobalAtlas/ predefinedReports/EFS2006/EFS_PDFs/EFS2006_GN.pdf) (PDF). World Health Organisation. 2006-12. . Retrieved 30 September 2007.

[46] https://www.cia.gov/library/publications/the-world-factbook/fields/2103.html

[47] Bureau of International Labor Affairs (ILAB) – U.S. Department of Labor (http://www.dol.gov/ilab/media/reports/iclp/tda2001/ guinea.htm). Dol.gov. Retrieved on 28 June 2011.

External links

- Official website (http://http://www.guinee.gov.gn) (French)
- Guinea (https://www.cia.gov/library/publications/the-world-factbook/geos/gv.html) entry at *The World Factbook*
- Guinea (http://www.dmoz.org/Regional/Africa/Guinea/) at the Open Directory Project
- Wikimedia Atlas of Guinea
- Guinea travel guide from Wikitravel
- The State of the World's Midwifery - Guinea Country Profile (http://www.unfpa.org/sowmy/resources/docs/ country_info/profile/en_GuineaC_SoWMy_Profile.pdf)

bjn:Guinea gag:Gvineya mrj:Гвиней

Temne language

Temne	
Spoken in	Central Sierra Leone
Native speakers	about 1,000,000.
Language family	Niger–Congo
	• Atlantic–Congo
	• Mel
	• Temne–Baga
	• **Temne**
Official status	
Regulated by	*No official regulation*
Language codes	
ISO 639-2	tem
ISO 639-3	tem

Temne (also known as 'Themne' or 'Timne', IPA: [ʈemnɛ]) is a language of the Atlantic subfamily of Niger–Congo languages spoken in Sierra Leone by about 2 million first speakers. One of the country's most widely spoken languages, it is spoken by 30% of the country's population. It also serves as a lingua franca for an additional 1,500,000 people living in areas near the Temne people. As a (West-)Atlantic language, Temne is relatively closely related to other well-known languages such as Fula (Fulfulde) and Wolof.

Temne is a tonal language, with four tones. It is related to the Baga languages spoken in Guinea and to Sherbro spoken in Sierra Leone. Temne speakers live mostly in the Northern Province and Western Area (Freetown and its environs) of Sierra Leone, Temne speakers can also be found in all 12 districts of Sierra Leone. Temne people can be found in a number of other West African countries as well, including Guinea and The Gambia. Some Temnes have also migrated beyond West Africa seeking educational and professional opportunities, especially in Great Britain, the United States, and Egypt. Temnes are mostly scholars, business people, farmers, and coastal fishermen; and most are Muslims.

Bibliography

* Bai-Sharka, Abou (1986) *Temne names and proverbs* [1] (Stories and songs from Sierra Leone vol. 19). Freetown: People's Educational Association of Sierra Leone.
* Turay, Abdul Karim (1989) *Temne stories*. Köln: Rüdiger Köppe Verlag.
* Wilson, W.A.A. (1961) *An outline of the Temne language*. London: University of London / SOAS.
* Yillah, M. Sorie (1992) *Temne phonology and morphology* [Unpublished thesis. New York: City University of New York]. Ann Arbor: UMI.

External links

- Temne on the Ethnologue [2]
- Temne Words and Phrases [3]
- CIA Sierra Leone file [4]
- PanAfrican L10n page on Temne [5]
- Listening example: Kassirie Stories [6]

References

[1] http://openlibrary.org/b/OL1583057M/Temne_names_and_proverbs

[2] http://www.ethnologue.com/show_language.asp?code=tem

[3] http://www.visitsierraleone.org/temne.asp

[4] https://www.cia.gov/library/publications/the-world-factbook/geos/sl.html#People

[5] http://www.panafril10n.org/wikidoc/pmwiki.php/PanAfrLoc/Temne

[6] http://ia360636.us.archive.org/1/items/Sierra_Leone_Stories/kassirie_stories_TEMNE.ogg

Atlantic languages

(West) Atlantic	
(geographical)	
Geographic distribution:	Westernmost Africa
Linguistic classification:	Niger–Congo
	• Atlantic–Congo
	• (West) Atlantic
Subdivisions:	Bak (northern)
	Senegambian (northern)
	Mel (southern)
	Limba (southern)
	Gola (southern)

The **Atlantic** or **West Atlantic languages**[1] of West Africa are an obsolete proposed major group of the Niger–Congo languages. They are those languages west of Kru which have the noun-class systems characteristic of the Niger–Congo family; in this they are distinguished from their Mande neighbors, which do not. The Atlantic languages are highly diverse and it is now generally accepted that they do not form a valid group. Linguists such as Dimmendahl, Blench, Hyman, and Segerer classify them into three or more independent branches of Niger–Congo. The term 'Atlantic languages' is kept as a geographic term of convenience.

The Atlantic languages are spoken along the Atlantic coast from Senegal to Liberia, though transhumant Fula speakers have spread eastward and are found in large numbers across the Sahel, from Senegal to Nigeria and Cameroon. Wolof of Senegal and several of the Fula languages are the most populous Atlantic languages, with several million speakers each; other significant members include Serer and the Jola dialect cluster of Senegal and Temne in Sierra Leone. The Northern Atlantic languages exhibit consonant mutation, and most Atlantic languages have noun-class systems similar to those of the distantly related Bantu languages. Some members are tonal, while others have pitch accent systems. The basic word order tends to be SVO.

Classification

The Atlantic family was first identified by Sigismund Koelle in 1854. In the early 20th century, Carl Meinhof claimed that Fula was a Hamitic language, but August von Klingenhaben and Joseph Greenberg's work conclusively established Fula's close relationship with Wolof and Serer. W. A. A. Wilson notes that the validity of the family as a whole rests on much weaker evidence, though it is clear that the languages are part of the Niger–Congo family, based on evidence such as a shared noun class system. However, comparative work on Niger–Congo is in its infancy. Classifications of Niger–Congo, usually based on lexicostatistics, generally propose that the Atlantic languages are rather divergent, but less so than Mande and other languages that lack noun classes.

David Sapir (1971) proposed a classification of Atlantic into three branches, a northern group (Northern Atlantic and Bak), a southern group (Mel, Limba, and Gola), and the divergent Bijago language of the Bissagos Islands off the coast of Guinea-Bissau (Wilson 1989). However, Segerer (2010), the only classification since Sapir, places Bijago together with the Bak languages; Bak, the rest of Northern (defined by consonant mutation), and Mel are independent branches in his view, and Gola and Limba Niger–Congo isolates.

Notes

[1] "West Atlantic" is the traditional term, following Diedrich Hermann Westermann; "Atlantic" is more typical in recent work, particularly since Bendor-Samuel (1989).

References

- Holst, Jan Henrik. "Reconstructing the mutation system of Atlantic." Neuried, 2008.
- Pozdniakov, Konstantin. "Etudes atlantiques comparatives : questions de méthodologie." Mémoires de la Société linguistique de Paris, XV, 2007, p. 93-119.
- Pozdniakov, Konstantin. "Problèmes de l'étude comparative historique des langues atlantiques". Sprache und Geschichte in Afrika, 2007.
- Pozdniakov, Konstantin & Segerer, Guillame. Tradition et rupture dans les grammaires comparées de différentes familles de langues », 2007, p. 93-119.
- Guillaume Serere & Florian Lionnet 2010. "'Isolates' in 'Atlantic'" (http://25images.ish-lyon.cnrs.fr/player/ player.php?id=72&id_sequence=431). *Language Isolates in Africa* workshop, Lyon, Dec. 4
- [author?] *Reconstruction des pronoms atlantiques et typologie des systèmes pronominaux // Systèmes de marques personnelles en Afrique.* Collection «Afrique et Langage », 8, 2004, p. 151-162.
- Sapir, David (1971). West Atlantic: An inventory of the languages, their noun class systems and consonant alternations. *Current Trends in Linguistics* 7:45-112. The Hague: Mouton.
- Wilson, W. A. A. (1989). Atlantic. In John Bendor-Samuel (Ed.), *The Niger–Congo Languages*, pp. 81–104.

External links

- Linguisitic and folklore material from Kujamaat Joola (http://etext.virginia.edu/african/Kujamaat/)
- UCLA page on Wolof (http://www.humnet.ucla.edu/humnet/aflang/Wolof/wolofInfo.html)
- Ethnologue report for Atlantic (http://www.ethnologue.com/show_family.asp?subid=89964)
- Journal of West African Languages: Atlantic languages (http://www.journalofwestafricanlanguages.org/ Atlantic.aspx)
- Konstantin Pozdniakov's personal site (http://pozdniakov.free.fr/index_fichiers/Page853.htm#comparativ)

Roger Blench

Roger Blench (born 1953) is a British linguist, ethnomusicologist and development anthropologist. He has an M.A. and a Ph.D. from the University of Cambridge and remains based in Cambridge, England. He actively researches and publishes, although he works as a private consultant rather than in academia.

A noted expert in African lingusitics,[1] Blench's main area of linguistic interest is the Niger–Congo language family although he has also researched the Nilo-Saharan and Afroasiatic families. He has also written about other language families and endangered languages. He has published extensively on the relationship between linguistics and archaeology, principally in Africa, but more recently also in East Asia. He is currently engaged in a long-term project to document the languages of Central Nigeria.

He collaborated extensively with the late Professor Kay Williamson, who died in January 2005, and is now a trustee of the Kay Williamson Educational Fund, which exists both to publish the unpublished material left by Kay Williamson and to promote the study of Nigerian languages. A series of publications supported by the trust is under way with Rüdiger Köppe Verlag in Cologne.

Blench has also conducted research and evaluations of international development activities worldwide, as a consultant and formerly as a research fellow of the Overseas Development Institute in London.

Books

- 1992. Crozier, D. H. & Blench, R. M. *An Index of Nigerian Languages.* Abuja: Language Development Centre; Ilorin: University of Ilorin; Dallas: SIL. ISBN 0-88312-611-7
- 1997. Blench, R. M. & Spriggs, M., eds. *Archaeology and Language I: theoretical and methodological orientations.* London: Routledge. ISBN 0-415-11760-7
- 1998. Blench, R. M. & Spriggs, M., eds. *Archaeology and Language II: correlating archaeological and linguistic hypotheses.* London: Routledge. ISBN 0-415-11761-5
- 1999a. Blench, R. M. & Spriggs, M., eds. *Archaeology and Language III: Artefacts, languages, and texts.* London: Routledge. ISBN 0-415-10054-2
- 1999b. Blench, R. M. & Spriggs, M., eds. *Archaeology and Language, IV: language change and cultural transformation.* London: Routledge. ISBN 0-415-11786-0
- 2000. Blench, R. M. & MacDonald, K. C., eds. *The Origin and Development of African Livestock.* London: University College Press.
- 2005. Sagart, L.; Blench, R. M. & Sanchez-Mazas, Alicia, eds. *The Peopling of East Asia.* London: Routledge. ISBN 0-415-32242-1
- 2006. *Archaeology, Language, and the African Past.* AltaMira Press. ISBN 0-759-10465-4
- 2008. Sanchez-Mazas, Alicia; Blench, R. M. et al., eds. *Human Migrations in Continental East Asia and Taiwan: matching archaeology, linguistics and genetics.* London: Routledge.

See also

- Indo-Pacific languages

References

[1] Review: [untitled] John Hewson Reviewed work(s): Archaeology, Language, and the African Past by Roger Blench Canadian Journal of African Studies Vol. 41, No. 3, http://www.jstor.org/stable/40380107

External links

- Roger Blench personal website (http://rogerblench.info/RBOP.htm)

Bijago language

Bijago	
Spoken in	Guinea-Bissau
Region	Offshore Bissagos Islands
Native speakers	30,000
Language family	Niger–Congo
	• Atlantic–Congo
	• Bak
	• **Bijago**
Language codes	
ISO 639-3	bjg

Bijago, or **Bidyogo**, is the language of the Bissagos Archipelago of Guinea-Bissau. There are some difficulties of grammar and intelligibility between dialects, with the Kamona dialect of Caravela and Carache Islands being unintelligible to the others.

Characteristics

The Kajoko dialect of Bijago is one of the few speech varieties of the world known to use a linguolabial consonant, the voiced stop [ɗ], in its basic sound system (Olson et al. in press).

Classification

Bijago is highly divergent. Sapir (1971) classified it as an isolate within the West Atlantic family. However, Segerer showed that this is primarily due to unrecognized sound changes, and that Bijago is in fact close to the Bak languages. For example, the following cognates in Bijago and Joola Kasa (a Bak language) are completely regular, but had not previously been identified (Serere 2010):

Gloss	Bijago	Joola Kasa
head	bu	fu-kow
eye	nɛ	ji-cil

References

- Olson, Kenneth S., D. William Reiman, Fernando Sabio & Filipe Alberto da Silva. In press. The voiced linguolabial plosive in Kajoko. Chicago Linguistic Society (CLS) 45(1).
- Segerer, Guillaume. La langue bijogo. Oxford : Pergamon Press, 1997.
- Segerer, Guillaume. L'origine des Bijogo : hypothèses de linguiste. In Gaillard, Gérald (Ed), Migrations anciennes et peuplement actuel des Côtes guinéennes, Paris : L'Harmattan, 2000, pp. 183–191
- Segerer, Guillaume. La langue bijogo de Bubaque (Guinée Bissau). Louvain, Paris : Editions Peeters, 2002. 310 pp.
- Guillaume Serere & Florian Lionnet 2010. "'Isolates' in 'Atlantic'". *Language Isolates in Africa* workshop, Lyon, Dec. 4

Baga languages

Baga	
Ethnicity:	Baga people
Geographic distribution:	coastal Guinea
Linguistic classification:	Niger–Congo
	• Atlantic–Congo
	• Mel
	• Temne
	• **Baga**
Subdivisions:	Landoma
	Baga proper

The **Baga languages** are five related languages spoken in the coastal region of Guinea by the Baga people. The total number of speakers of Baga languages is about 30,000, of which the Landoma speakers make up almost 50 %. Most of the Baga are bilingual in the Mande language Susu, the official regional language. Two Baga communities are known to have abandoned their language altogether in favour of Susu, namely the Sobané and Kaloum.

Four of the five varieties still spoken are sometimes considered dialects of one language, *Baga* or *Barka*. The name is derived from the phrase *bae raka*, 'people of the seaside'. Landoma is classified as a Baga language, but is somewhat more distantly related to the other four languages. The Baga languages are related to Temne, one of the four official languages of Sierra Leone; together, Baga and Temne belong to the Mel branch of Niger–Congo languages.

- Baga Binari (Binari)
- Baga Koga (Koba)
- Baga Manduri (Maduri, Mandari).
- Baga Sitemu (Sitemú, Stem Baga, Rio Pongo Baga).
- Landoma (Landuma, Landouman, Tyapi)

Bibliography

- Houis, Maurice (1952) 'Remarques sur la voix passive en Baga', *Notes Africaines*, 91–92.
- Houis, Maurice (1953) 'Le système pronominal et les classes dans les dialectes Baga, i carte', *Bulletin de l'IFAN*, 15, 381–404.
- Mouser, Bruce L. (2002) 'Who and where were the Baga?: European perceptions from 1793 to 1821', *History in Africa*, 29, 337–364.

External links

- The Baga branch on the Ethnologue [1]

References

[1] http://www.ethnologue.com/show_family.asp?subid=92257

Bullom languages

Bullom	
Geographic distribution:	coastal Guinea

Linguistic classification:	Niger–Congo
	• Atlantic–Congo
	  • Mel
	    • Bullom–Kisi
	      • **Bullom**

Subdivisions:	—

The **Bullom languages** are a small group of Mel languages spoken in Sierra Leone. The languages are Bom, Bullom So (Mmani), Sherbro, and Krim. They are closely related to Kissi.

Article Sources and Contributors

Mel languages *Source*: http://en.wikipedia.org/w/index.php?title=Limba%E2%80%93Mel_languages *Contributors*: Kwamikagami, 3 anonymous edits

Mel languages *Source*: http://en.wikipedia.org/w/index.php?title=Limba%E2%80%93Mel_languages *Contributors*: Kwamikagami, 3 anonymous edits

Niger–Congo languages *Source*: http://en.wikipedia.org/w/index.php?title=Niger-Congo_languages *Contributors*: ABF, Abiola Lapite, Aleichem, Anak 1, Andre Engels, Andrew Dalby, Aranel, Awuka, Banaticus, Bidabadi, Blake3522, Bletch, Bryan Derksen, Burschik, Bws2002, Calypso, Chrajohn, Christian Historybuff, Circeus, Cmsg, Colonies Chris, Conversion script, Cyryllo, Darwinek, Davidcannon, Demmy, Diderot, Doyley, Dvyost, Ectoplasmer, Elium2, Evlekis, Ezeu, FilipeS, Flatterworld, GCarty, Gailtb, Gaius Cornelius, Garzo, Grandmasterka, Guaka, Gunjan verma81, Halaqah, Hannes Hirzel, Hippietrail, Hirzel, Hollah, Iketsi, Ish ishwar, Jfarrell4, John K, Jorge Stolfi, JorisvS, Joziboy, Karl-Henner, Kazvorpal, Koryakov Yuri, Kwamikagami, Ligulem, Liotier, LokiClock, MacedonianBoy, Macrakis, MarcoAurelio, Mark Dingemanse, Marquetry28, Martin.Budden, Mboverload, Meekywiki, Mel Etitis, Montrealais, Moswento, Munci, Mustafaa, Nannus, Notscott, Olivier, Otto ter Haar, Palnatoke, Pekinensis, Pgdudda, R'n'B, RJFJR, Rgoodermote, Rich Farmbrough, Rjwilmsi, Ruakh, Saforrest, Shanes, Sheynhertz-Unbayg, Silverxxx, Smaines, Stephan Schulz, Strangeloop, T L Miles, Taivo, TenPoundHammer, Timothy Usher, Tommy2010, Toussaint, Ukabia, VeryVerily, VikSol, Virginia-American, WikiMarshall, Woohookitty, Xx236, Yamlikha, Yom, Zyxoas, 94 anonymous edits

Guinea-Bissau *Source*: http://en.wikipedia.org/w/index.php?title=Guinea-Bissau *Contributors*: *drew, -- April, 2help, A Werewolf, A-giau, A12n, A2Kafir, Aaker, Abeldjassi, Abigail alderate, Acntx, Adam Carr, Adrianbrodal, Aecharri, Aflis, Aflm, Againme, Ahoerstemeier, Ajbpearce, Akanemoto, Alan Liefting, AlefZet, Alex45, AlexanderKaras, Andy Marchbanks, Angr, AnnaFrance, Aordictator, Aotearoa, Arnkristen, Astanhope, Asterion, Attilios, B00P, BDD, Banhtrung1, Baraqa1, Bash, Bazonka, Belovedfreak, Bigturtle, BillFlis, Bissau777, Blaineeee, Bobblewik, Borgx, Briaboru, Buaidh, Bugo30, CWesling, Cajetan da kid, Cam, Camarinha, Cameroony11, Cantus, Caponer, CarlKenner, Cattus, Cburnett, Cdc, Ceyockey, Cimon Avaro, Cjs, Colonies Chris, CommonsDelinker, Conte di Cavour, Conversion script, Corvus13, Crusio, Cshobe, CultureDrone, Cwolfsheep, D6, DARTH SIDIOUS 2, DTR, Danger, DanielCD, Dark Shikari, Davehi1, David Kernow, Dbenbenn, Ddama, Debutante, Deflective, Demicx, Demmy, DerHexer, Dewan357, DiiCinta, Diogo sfreitas, DivineIntervention, Dogaroon, Domaleixo, Domino theory, Dr. Blofeld, Drbug, Dubhe.sk, Ducat1base, Dvalerio, Dyersgoodness, E Pluribus Anthony, Eastlaw, El C, Emijrp, EncycloPetey, Enigmaman, Eranb, Everyking, Evil Monkey, FayssalF, Feydey, Flatterworld, Flewis, Forresj1, Fram, Frankie816, GMMarques, GRUM75, Gadfium, Gauss, Ggggh, GhostPirate, Gilliam, Glenn L, Golbez, Good Olfactory, Goustien, Gr8opinionater, Graham87, Green Giant, Grendelkhan, Gryffindor, Gurch, Gznorneplatz, Gzornenplatz, Haporuk, HeikoEvermann, Hirpex, Hmains, Hux, Hypnosadist, I think 2 + 2 = 22., IJA, Ief, Iketsi, IkonicDeath, Ipod Upod Weallpod, IronGargoyle, Istanbuljohnm, J04n, JamesR, Janko, JerryFriedman, Jhendin, Jherrity, Jiang, Jkp1187, Joaopais, John Lunney, John Z, JohnLease, Jojit fb, Jomifica, Jonkerz, Jorge Stolfi, JorgeGG, Jorunn, Jose77, Joseph Solis in Australia, Juliancolton, Jusjih, Kaldari, Kanags, Karakatoa, Kate, Kevin Rector, Khoikhoi, Kintetsubuffalo, Klosterdev, Kman665, Knutux, Kotniski, Koyaanis Qatsi, KoyaanisQatsi, Kralizec!, Kristjan Wager, Kupecap, Kwamikagami, Lakema, Larissakir, Liftarn, Lightmouse, Limongi, Luis wiki, Luizdl, Lupin, MECU, MINGESELLE821, MJCdetroit, MJD86, Man vyi, Mandacuva, Manuel de Sousa, Mapryan, Marek69, Marktreut, Martinwilke1980, Martpol, Matthew Fennell, Mattisse, Maurreen, Mayita1usa, McDogm, Mcornils, Miaow Miaow, Mic, Middayexpress, Middleasternguy, Miranda, Montrealais, Moshe Constantine Hassan Al-Silverburg, Mr Stephen, Mr.Z-man, Mrdie, Muhammad Daffa Rambe, Muhandes, Munci, Mushroom, Mário, Narayansg, NatalieF25, NawlinWiki, Neumannk, Night w, Nightstallion, Nono64, Notheruser, Nricardo, Numbo3, Ohnoitsjamie, Oren neu dag, Parakalo, Pascal, Paul Benjamin Austin, PedroPVZ, Peruvianllama, Peter Horn, PeterisP, Petrux, Peyre, PhilKnight, Philip Cross, PimRijkee, Polaron, Polylerus, Potatoswatter, Presidentman, Profoss, Pteron, Purpleturple, Qrfqr, Quadell, Questchest, Railwayman, Rarelibra, Red Winged Duck, Remigiu, Revent99, Reverendlinux, Reywas92, Rich Farmbrough, Richard Trillo, Rick Block, Rjwilmsi, Rmpfu89, Roke, Roksanna, Romanm, Rose Garden, Royalrec, Rvknight, S. Randall, SFC9394, SGGH, Saalstin, Saforrest, Samantha555, Sarcelles, Saulopro, Schaengel89, Scipius, Scott Illini, SeNeKa, Seb az86556, Secfan, Sesel, Sharn-Lugonn, SheepNotGoats, Sillyfolkboy, SimonP, SisuUnlimited, Skinsmoke, Skrofler, Slightsmile, Sluzzelin, Snottily, SpaceRocket, SpyMagician, Stan Shebs, Suruena, Sven70, T L Miles, TAG-A-b10, TCB007, TUF-KAT, TXiKi, Tabletop, Taivo, Tanketz, Taospark, Tempestman2, Template namespace initialisation script, TenIslands, TexasDawg, ThaGrind, The Epopt, The Ogre, The Transhumanist, The monkeyhate, TheEditrix2, Therequiembellishere, ThomasK, Thricecube, Tibullus, Tim Starling, TintininLisbon, Tired time, Tpbradbury, Travelbird, Truco, Tugaworld, Uncle Milty, Unyoyega, Vardion, Velho, VillaVertigo, VinnyCee, Vitorsba, Vlma111, VoodooIsland, Waldir, Warofdreams, Wavelength, WhisperToMe, Wik, Willem Tijssen, Wiwaxia, Wizzy, Wjh, Wkharrisjr, Wragge, Wyllium, Xed, YCM Interista, Yolanda12, Yu210148, Zebaba, Zscout370, Саша Стефановић, 268 anonymous edits

Sierra Leone *Source*: http://en.wikipedia.org/w/index.php?title=Sierra_Leone *Contributors*: (jarbarf), *bj*, *drew, 11844a, 1297, 21655, 334a, 7h3 h4x0r, A F K When Needed, A Werewolf, A-giau, A12n, ABF, Aadavalus, Abberley2, Abdiali14, AbhijayM., Ablyall, AbsolutDan, Aceleo, Ackees, Acntx, Acs4b, Adam murgittroyd, Addshore, Adrianbrodal, Adsgiii, Affanwasim, Aflm, AgnosticPreachersKid, Ahoerstemeier, Airsplit, Aitias, Ajcheema, Akanemoto, Al Ameer son, Alan Liefting, Alansohn, Ale jrb, Aleenf1, AlefZet, Alexandru Stanoi, AlexiusHoratius, Alexr92, Alieu99, All As One, Allanp5, Alma Hadzic, Aluspha, Ammon86, Analogue Kid, Andrew H. Goldberg, AndrewHowse, Andrewpmk, Andy Marchbanks, Andy4789, Anetode, Angryafghan, Angrymansr, Ank0ku, Anonymous Dissident, Antandrus, Aridd, ArielGold, Arsonal, Arthena, Arx Fortis, Asmunda, AssistantEditorsBro, Astrotrain, Attilios, Aude, Auntof6, Avala, Avaneeshk, Avg, Avs5221, Azrail911, BD2412, Bahamut Star, Balletballet, BanyanTree, Barliner, Baronnet, BarretBonden, BartlebyScrivener, BaseballDetective, Basicdesign, Basilisk4u, Bawtyshouse, Bazonka, BeeTea, Behemoth, Bellagio99, Belovedfreak, Bemoeial, Ben Ben, BenitaE, Bgpaulus, Bidabadi, Biruitorul, Bk0, Bkell, Black Kite, Bleff, Bletch, Blikes, Blood Red Sandman, Bluezy, Bobblehead, Bobblewik, Bobfreshwater, Bobo192, Bobrayner, Bokpasa, Bonadea, Bossede, Brainhell, BrainyBabe, Briaboru, Brian-fca, Bridesmill, Brotha-x, Bruce1ee, Brutannica, Bruxism, Buaidh, Bubba hotep, Bucksburg, Buckshot06, Buickid, Bulwersator, Butchdaulton, Bwob, C toney, CIreland, CJ, CalicoCatLover, Caltas, Can't sleep, clown will eat me, Canley, Cantus, Caponer, Captain-tucker, CaptinJohn, CarlKenner, CasperDiamante, CastformRED, Cburnett, Cdc, ChanDMan2010, Chanheigeorge, Charles Paxton, CharlotteWebb, Chensiyuan, Chiefmagoo, Childzy, Chipuni, Chris the speller, Chrism, Chtrede, Ciand, Ciotog, Clam0p, Clarkbark, Closedmouth, Codex Sinaiticus, Coffee, Colinfitz8, Collinw23, CommonsDelinker, Condem, Congolese fufu, Conte di Cavour, Conversion script, Cooperh, Cop 663, Corpx, Corriebertus, Cotoco, Countcows, Cresix, Crusio, Csobankai Aladar, Ctbolt, Curtbash, Cwolfsheep, D, D Code-40, DARTH SIDIOUS 2, DSRH, Damifb, Danger, Danielpantzhero, Danny, Darwinek, Dave1959, Dave6, David Kernow, David Newton, David.cormier, Davidcannon, Dawkeye, Dawn Bard, Dbfirs, Dblecros, Dcalfine, Dcghjsfdhg, Deametwork, Debresser, Deflective, Deiz, Delldot, Delta56, Demicx, Denis C., Deor, Der Falke, DerHexer, Deville, Difu Wu, DirkvdM, Discospinster, DivineIntervention, Docu, Doldrums, Domaleixo, Donald Albury, Dr who1975, Drakons, Drbug, Dsp13, Dthomsen8, Du2007du, Dubhe.sk, Duwenbasden, ESkog, EamonnPKeane, Edgar181, Editore99, Efghij, Egyptoo, El C, El KG, El Simbo, Electionworld, Elektronen, Elockid, EncycloPetey, Enlil Ninlil, Enterwayevents, Enviroboy, Epbr123, Ersutton1, Erudy, EscapingLife, Eumolpo, Everyking, EvilCouch, ExitRight, Ezeu, F Notebook, FERN EU, FF2010, Factmon, Fdewaele, Felixboy, FilipeS, Fixer88, Fjarlq, Flatterworld, Flewis, Flosssock1, Flyguy649, Fogster, Foufo, Fraggle81, Fratrep, FruitywS, Fuera, Funandtrvl, Funnyhat, Furrykef, Fuzheado, GB fan, GRUM75, Gaius Cornelius, Gantry, Garzo, Geni, Geowolfe, GerardM, Gggh, Giftlite, GigidyG, Gilliam, Gkklein, Glacier Wolf, Gobobo, Gobonobo, Gogo Dodo, GoingBatty, Goldfishbutt, Goldintheair, Gomez2002, Gonzonoir, Good Olfactory, Gorgan almighty, Gr8opinionater, GraemeL, Graham87, Greatal386, Green Giant, GregorB, Grendelkhan, Grunty Thraveswain, Gryffindor, Gurch, Gutho, Gyrofrog, HRights, Hadal, Hakluyt bean, Halaqah, Hamamelis, Happy-melon, HappyArtichoke, Happydog123, Harry Potter, Harryboyles, HartleyHare, Haseo9999, Hashar, Hdt83, Heegoop, HeikoEvermann, Highfields, Hmains, Hoplon, HornetMike, Hottentot, Huhsunqu, Hungrycookpot, Hunocsi, Hut 8.5, Hydrogen Iodide, IJA, Icestorm815, Idrinktoomuch, Ief, IitocSakas, Ilikepie2221, Ilikerap416, Ilyushka88, Impaciente, IntrigueBlue, IronGargoyle, Isfisk, Ishikawa Minoru, Istanbuljohnm, Itai, Iulus Ascanius, Iwanttoeditthissh, J.delanoy, JForget, JYi, Jahangard, JamesAM, JamesBWatson, Jarry1250, Jarvoll, Jason526, Jauerback, Jayman75, Jdkoenig, Jebba, Jeeny, Jefe2000, Jeff G., Jeff Silvers, Jeff3000, Jeronimo, Jhendin, Jiang, Jkoenj, JoSePh, JoeSmack, John Cardinal, John Foxe, John Kwame, John of Reading, Jojit fb, JonC0001, Jonathan O'Donnell, Jonkerz, Jonmwang, Jophus00, Jorge Stolfi, Jorunn, Jose77, Joshays, Jossi, Jpgordon, Justinep, Jwillbur, KDS4444, Kajerm, Kaly99, KariLaneB, Karin62, Kday, Kdehl, Keegan, Kellogg257, Kevin Baas, Kevinpurcell, Kevspencer, Khazar, Khfan93, Kim Williams, Kintetsubuffalo, Kitkatcrazy, Kiwi100, Kman665, KnowledgeOfSelf, Knutux, Korbannc, Kotniski, Koyaanis Qatsi, KoyaanisQatsi, Kpjas, Kralizec!, Krich, Kschwerdt514, Ktsquare, Kurt Jansson, Kurvjuh, Kwamikagami, Kwsn, L0b0t, LILK1998, La la ooh, Laddiebuck, Law, Le Fou, LeoNomis, Leutha, Levineps, Lfc112, Lfh, Lightmouse, Lihaas, LilHelpa, Lime turtwig, Limongi, LittleRoughRhinestone, Ljhliesl, Llamapez, Londonlnd, LookatLao, Lotje, Luk, Luke-simmons, Lupin, M.W.A., M100, M3taphysical, MER-C, MJCdetroit, MJD86, MJohnson0, Mabuhelwa, Macrit, Macronyx, Maelnuneb, Magic.Wiki, Maksim L., Malhonen, Malinaccier, Mancunius, Manway, Marixist101, Mark Dingemanse, Mark Ryan, MarkS, MarkVolundNYC, Marshallsumter, Martyn50, Marwan123, Masur, Math Champion, Matthew Fennell, Mattisse, Mattop123, Mav, Maxi danger, Mayz, Mbc362, Mboverload, McDogm, McSly, McTrixie, Mcg410, Mdp22, Merbabu, Mervyn, Mic, Michael Johnson, Michaeltobbylee, Michellecrisp, Mickey gfss2007, Micro01, Middayexpress, Mike Halterman, Mild Bill Hiccup, Mini-Geek, MinnesotanConfederacy, Mistervandelay, Mkurz2, Mlc409, Mmxx, Monkipuzzle, Montrealais, Moonriver90, Mouat, Mouse is back, Mschiffler, Msrasnw, Mtking, Muctay, Munci, Murderbike, Musichick182, Muzza45, N5iln, NJW494, Nadinedahab, Namiba, Naomi smith, Natsubee, Nausea, NawlinWiki, Ndlfutbol1, Neelix, NeilN, Netknowle, Neurophysics, NewEnglandYankee, Nickshanks, Nickwolf, NielsenGW, Night w, Nightstallion, Nishkid64, Nivix, No. 38.27, Noah Salzman, Noctibus, NorthernThunder, Notheruser, Nyttend, Ohconfucius, Ohnoitsjamie, Olivier, Omicronpersei8, Onorem, Orphan Wiki, Oscabat, Oscarthecat, Osomec, Ouedbirdwatcher, Overfed1, Oxymoron83, P M Yonge, PDH, PFHLai, PMLawrence, Packcigs, Padraic, Paine Ellsworth, Pais, Papaboymedia, Patinthehat1, Patrick-br, Paul Erik, Paul-L, Paul84, Pchief, Pdfpdf, Pedantic Peasant-hater, Pejorative.majeure, PenguiN42, Peter Horn, Peter morrell, Petestud3, Petuniafish, Peyre, Pgan002, Pharaoh of the Wizards, Phatenz, Pherve, Philip Baird Shearer, Philip Trueman, Pinethicket, Pink!Teen, Plexust, Pocketfox, Poetaris, PokemonPowerRanger, Polaron, Polluxian, Polylerus, Prayerfortheworld, Profoss, Pseudo-Richard, Pteron, Punkishlyevil, PyroTom, Pyrospirit, QWerk, QueenCake, Quiensabe, Quinsareth, Qurqa, Qwyrxian, R'n'B, RB972, RFerreira, RainbowOfLight, Rakim126, Rambler24, Random User 937494, RandomP, Rarelibra, Rashad9607, Ratibgreat, Ratzd'mishukribo, Razorflame, Rd232, Realrick7, Regancy42, Renata3, RexNL, Rhone, Rich Farmbrough, Rich257, Richard D. LeCour, Richard Trillo, Rick Block, Rickard Vogelberg, Rigadoun, Rivertorch, Rjwilmsi, RoadTrain, Roastytoast, RobinHood70, Robogun, Rodhullandemu, Rokfaith, Romanm, Ronald W Wise, Rory096, Royboycrashfan, Rrburke, SL992, SQGibbon, Sadalmelik, Salone-bby, Salonewatchman, Sam Hocevar, Sam Korn, Samantha555, Samuel Blanning, Sandstein, Sannse, Saranghae honey, Sarcelles, Sassf, Savant13, Schoolicion, Schrodinger's cat is alive, SchuminWeb, Scipius, Scoopczar, Scope creep, ScottDavis, Screamatkids145, Scythian1, Sdrtirs, Sean.hoyland, SeanMack, Seb az86556, Sebjarod, Secfan, Ser Amantio di Nicolao, Serte, Sesquina1, Sfrostee, Shadow1, Shadowjams, ShakataGaNai, Shalaleon, Shalom Yechiel, Shapsteve, SheepNotGoats, Shoessss, ShweNyarThar, Sierraleon, Simmid3093, SimonP, Simulacrist, Sinhala freedom, Sionus, Sittaconde, Sjorford, Skinsmoke, SkyWalker, Skyezx, Slawter500, Slipslap, Slowking Man, Sluzzelin, Smash505, Smmhyder, Smmurphy, Snowdog, Snowdrop44, Snowmanradio, Snoyes, Soler97, Some jerk on the Internet, Someone65, Spastiche, Spectacgurl215, SpikeToronto, Spitfire, Splaty, SpookyMulder, Springnuts, Srleffler, Sstrader, Stackp2, Starsimon, SteinbDJ, Stephen G. Brown, Steve G, Steven J. Anderson, Steveo1218, Sting au, Surpluzrage, Suva, SuzanneKn, Sven70, Swatjester, Swattie, Swedish fusilier, Szarka, T L Miles, THEN WHO WAS PHONE?, TUF-KAT, TaSluder6, Tabletop, Talkie tim, Taospark, Taschenrechner, TashiD, Tayedot, Tbhotch, Tedius Zanarukando,

Tellyaddict, Template namespace initialisation script, Tempodivalse, Terry J. Carter, The Anome, The Epopt, The Rambling Man, The Random Editor, The Thing That Should Not Be, The Transhumanist, The Universe Is Cool, TheGunn, TheIntersect, TheMadBaron, TheTito, Thehelpfulone, TheoloJ, Thiseye, ThorstenNY, Thricecube, Thucydides411, Tide rolls, Timbobutcher, Timeover8, Tired time, Titoxd, Tkynerd, Tocino, Tollbahn, Tomeasy, Tony1, Trotski99, Tvh2k, Tymichuky, Ubardak, Underlying Ik, UnicornTapestry, Updater25, Utcursch, Vanjagenije, Vardion, Varlet16, VartanM, Verne Equinox, Versus22, Violetriga, VityUvieu, Vlma111, VoodooIsland, Vortexrealm, Vrenator, Vssun, WATP, Waggers, WarthogDemon, Wasbeer, Wavelength, Welsh, WhisperToMe, Whoisjohngalt, WikHead, Wiki alf, WikiLaurent, WikiTome, Wikiaddict8962, Willem Tijssen, WithGLEE, Woohookitty, Wuapinmon, Wyllium, Wysprgr2005, X-up, Xagent86, Xdamr, Xenon54, Xnuala, Xushi, Xxalannahbananaxx, Xxpor, Yaatri, Yamamoto Ichiro, Yamara, YixifTesiphon, Youkai no unmei, Zachie, Zafiroblue05, Ziggy3055, Zntrip, Zoe, Zscout370, Île flottante, Саша Стефановић, 3470 anonymous edits

Guinea *Source*: http://en.wikipedia.org/w/index.php?title=Guinea *Contributors*: -- April, 0, 172, 28bytes, 7D HMS, A Werewolf, A-giau, A12n, Aaker, Acntx, Adamrush, Adrianbrodal, Ahoerstemeier, Aitias, Akanemoto, Alan Liefting, Alansohn, Alantauber, AlefZet, Alex460, Aluspha, Ammon86, Andy Marchbanks, AndySimpson, Antandrus, Applecider42, Aptenodytes, Art LaPella, Arthena, Attilios, Aude, Aupif, Auranor, Avala, Awkwaffle, Badagnani, Bahoumar, Bambipig, Banhtrung1, Baronnet, Bart133, Bassbonerocks, Bazonka, Bearcat, Begoon, Beland, Bemoeial, Bender235, Bentogoa, Bhadani, Bhoy Wonder, Bigturnip, Biruitorul, Bkavanaugh, Blanchardb, BobKawanaka, Bobblewik, Bobbo, Bobo192, Boubah, Boundacouda, Bradrogersau, Briaboru, BrianAdler, Bryan Derksen, Buaidh, Buchanan-Hermit, Buckshot06, Buddy431, CalistaA, Caltas, CambridgeBayWeather, Can't sleep, clown will eat me, Canadian Bobby, Cantus, Caponer, Catgut, Cburnett, Challenor, Chaosdruid, Cherry blossom tree, Chimin 07, Chipmunkdavis, Chris Latour, Chrism, Chuunen Baka, Cjs2111, Ckatz, Closedmouth, Cnilep, CommonsDelinker, Conte di Cavour, Conversion script, Corriebertus, Corvus13, Coyr, Craitman17, Credema, CultureDrone, Cwolfsheep, Cybercobra, Cyrus Andiron, Cyryllo, D6, DMG413, DO'Neil, Danger, Danny, Dannyreb, Darth Panda, DarwinPeacock, David Kernow, David.Mestel, Dayewalker, Dayg1110, Dbfirs, Deflective, Demicx, Demmy, DerHexer, DivineIntervention, Do go be man, Docu, Domaleixo, Donald Albury, Dputig07, Dr. Blofeld, Drbreznjev, Drbug, Drew R. Smith, Dubhe.sk, Duncan1800, Dvyost, E Pluribus Anthony, E2eamon, Editor2423, Ejercito Rojo 1967, El C, Elbasan101, Electionworld, EncycloPetey, Encyclopedist, Enlil Ninlil, Epbr123, Eranb, Ersutton1, Euzpr, Everyking, Evlekis, Ezeu, Facts707, Falc, Falcon8765, Farazy, Farolif, Fastcomp, FayssalF, Fconaway, Fieldday-sunday, Filletti, Firham74, Flarkins, Flatterworld, Fluffernutter, Flyboy121, Fram, Fry1989, Fusionsnake, GRUM75, Gail, Gaius Cornelius, Garfield226, GaryScheister, Garzo, Gazaki, Geni, Gggh, Ghytydrtuyu, Giamlarrahan, Gilliam, Gisaster25, Gobonobo, Gogo Dodo, Golbez, Good Olfactory, GraemeL, Graham87, Green Giant, Greenman, Grendelkhan, Grinman, Gryffindor, Gtdp, Guptan99, Gznomeplatz, Gzornenplatz, Hall Monitor, Hambuker0, Hansonw, Headhitter, Hebrides, HeikoEvermann, Heimstern, Hephaestos, Hertz1888, Hibernian, Hottentot, Howcheng, Hut 8.5, I m evil 123, I think 2 + 2 = 22., IJA, Iamsano, Iamsomean, Iancaddy, Idaltu, Ief, Ignacio Bibcraft, Ikiroid, Illnab1024, Imoen44, IndulgentReader, Io Katai, Ionius Mundus, IronGargoyle, Island Monkey, Istanbuljohnm, Iwanttoedithissh, J.delanoy, J04n, JDspeeder1, JForget, Jackblackcrack, Jake Wartenberg, JamesBWatson, JamesR, Jameslove, Jan Eduard, Jay-Sebastos, Jeroen, Jhendin, Jhenry4, Jimmosan, Jleske, Joao, Joelguinea, John K, Jojhutton, Jojit fb, Jomifica, JonC0001, Jonverve, Jorunn, Jose77, Joseph Solis in Australia, Joshua Scott, Joshuabowman, Jovinjoy, Jpatokal, Jpkoester1, Jsimpson1100, Julius Sahara, Justacityboy, KJS77, Katalaveno, Kcarr1993, Keilana, Khoikhoi, Kimdime, Kintetsubuffalo, Kiwadian, Kjkolb, Knopffabrik, Knutux, Kotniski, Koulibaly, Koyaanis Qatsi, Kritikos99, Ktsquare, Kwamikagami, L Kensington, LFaraone, LarryQ, Legra61, LeilaniLad, Leonard^Bloom, Lexicon, Lfh, Lfstevens, LiDaobing, Lightmouse, Lilaac, Lilac Soul, Limongi, Long9johnson, Loren.wilton, Lotje, Luna Santin, Lupin, M.O.X, MFH, MINGESELLE299, MINGESELLE821, MJCdetroit, MJD86, Malhonen, Malik Shabazz, Mandarax, Manfi, ManicParroT, Margezze, Mark R Johnson, Martianmister, Martin tamb, Martiniano, Martinwilke1980, Mashford, Master Jay, Mattisse, MauriManya, Mbility, McTrixie, Mentifisto, Miaow Miaow, Mic, Michael Hardy, Middayexpress, Midway, Mikm, Milkbreath, Mitch1981, Mitchrice, Mizztb09, Mohamedkaba, Moncrief, Moose1794, Morwen, Mr.Z-man, Mschiffler, Mtwstudios, Muhammad Daffa Rambe, MusicMaker5376, Mxn, Myanw, NAHID, Nabla, Naddy, Nakon, Nalco, Namiba, NatalieF25, Natsubee, NawlinWiki, Nealmcb, Nebuchadnezzar o'neill, NellieBly, Neneboho, NeoChaosX, New4325, Nick-D, NickVertical, Night w, Nightstallion, Nono64, Not the maximum, Notheruser, Numbo3, Nwbeeson, Nygdan, Nyttend, Ohconfucius, Ohnoitsjamie, Oneanddone, Opbeith, Orangemike, Oren neu dag, Oxymoron83, PMDrive1061, PTJoshua, Pascal, Patrick-br, Patstuart, Paul August, Paul Erik, Pearle, Peter Horn, PeterisP, Petrux, Peyre, Pgan002, Philip Trueman, Picaroon, Pie lover123, Pink Bull, Polaron, Polylerus, Porturology, Possum, Ppearson, Prari, Prodego, Profoss, Prolog, Prvc, Psycho Squirrel 11, PsychoPiglet, Pteron, Pyrrhon8, Quackslikeaduck, Quigley, Qutezuce, Qwyrxian, R'n'B, R0pe-196, RadiantRay, Random contributor, RandomCritic, RapidR, Rarelibra, Raven4x4x, Raymondwinn, Recognizance, Red King, Red Winged Duck, Redmarkviolinist, Reedy, Regis dumoulin, Renaissancee, Rich Farmbrough, Richard D. LeCour, Richard Trillo, Richard Weil, Rick Block, Rif Winfield, Rizalninoynapoleon, Rjwilmsi, RoadTrain, Rob Lindsey, RockMFR, Romanm, Ronk01, Rose Garden, Rowinator, Rudolfhess456, Ryan, Rydia, SDC, SFC9394, SPQRobin, Sabine's Sunbird, Saforrest, Sam Hocevar, Sam ware, Samantha555, Samjanssen, Sarcelles, Schaengel89, Scipius, Scythian1, Scythian99, SeanMack, Seb az86556, Secfan, Ser Amantio di Nicolao, Serpent's Choice, Sesel, Shalom Yechiel, SimonP, Sinhala freedom, SisuUnlimited, Sittaconde, Sleigh, Slo186, Sluzzelin, Smartse, Smeds, Snowdog, Soman, Soulbah, SparrowsWing, Spitfire19, SpookyMulder, Steffler, Stan En, SteinbDJ, Steinbach, Stephen Gilbert, Storm Rider, Stunetii, SusanLesch, Sven70, Sw258, T L Miles, THEunique, TUF-KAT, TXiKi, Tabletop, Talon Artaine, Tanthalas39, Taospark, TehMightyButters, Telerhythm, Template namespace initialisation script, Tempodivalse, Terrek, The High Fin Sperm Whale, The Transhumanist, TheEditrix2, Therequiembellishere, ThinkEnemies, Thiseye, Thnidu, Thomas Larsen, Thricecube, Tide rolls, Timbobutcher, Tobby72, Tobias Conradi, Tomdobb, Tommy Kronkvist, Tpbradbury, Trengarasu, Tresiden, Trevor MacInnis, TwoOneTwo, Tyfighter0, Uiscefada, Uncle G, Uncle798, Unschool, Valstina, Vardion, Versus22, Vinger, VityUvieu, Vlma111, VoodooIsland, Voyagerfan5761, Vssun, WadeSimMiser, Washburnmav, Wefkin.Shibboleth, WhisperToMe, Widsith, Wik, WikiHendrik, Wikiaddict8962, Wikisteve12, Wikiwikisteve2, Woodyteegra, Woohookitty, Wyllium, Xed, Xiglofre, Yahel Guhan, Yamamoto Ichiro, Yancyfry jr, Yellowdesk, Yom, Youssefsan, Yug, Yvesnimmo, Zscout370, Саша Стефановић, 827 anonymous edits

Temne language *Source*: http://en.wikipedia.org/w/index.php?title=Temne_language *Contributors*: A12n, Babbage, Badagnani, Baishek, Garzo, Ionius Mundus, Joseph opala, Kikos, Kwamikagami, Lgeneh, Mark Dingemanse, Moyogo, Omnipaedista, Skinsmoke, 18 anonymous edits

Atlantic languages *Source*: http://en.wikipedia.org/w/index.php?title=Atlantic_languages *Contributors*: Angr, Black Falcon, Burschik, CRGreathouse, Charles Matthews, Chrajohn, Edricson, Ewulp, Grutness, Hirzel, Hraefen, J. 'mach' wust, Kwamikagami, Llydawr, Malhonen, Mark Dingemanse, Mellery, Mustafaa, Neelix, Nicke L, RGravina, Rmhermen, RoySmith, Tropylium, Woohookitty, 8 anonymous edits

Roger Blench *Source*: http://en.wikipedia.org/w/index.php?title=Roger_Blench *Contributors*: Aeusoes1, Bearcat, Circeus, Dekimasu, Epbr123, Felix Folio Secundus, Fleebo, Kwamikagami, Linguistic Science, Mandarax, Mark Dingemanse, Marm, Medeis, Pacific Archaeologist, Reaverdrop, Retired username, Stevenmitchell, Zahir Mgeni, 14 anonymous edits

Bijago language *Source*: http://en.wikipedia.org/w/index.php?title=Bijago_language *Contributors*: Avicennasis, Demmy, Huttarl, Iketsi, Jon Harald Søby, Kwamikagami, Ser Amantio di Nicolao, 1 anonymous edits

Baga languages *Source*: http://en.wikipedia.org/w/index.php?title=Baga_languages *Contributors*: Carabinieri, Dominus Vobisdu, Kwamikagami, MaGa, Man vyi, Mark Dingemanse, P h1999, RHaworth, T L Miles, Yayaban, 4 anonymous edits

Bullom languages *Source*: http://en.wikipedia.org/w/index.php?title=Bullom_languages *Contributors*: Kwamikagami

Image Sources, Licenses and Contributors

File:Niger-Congo.svg *Source*: http://en.wikipedia.org/w/index.php?title=File:Niger-Congo.svg *License*: unknown *Contributors*: AnonMoos, Jon Harald Søby, Kimdime, Moyogo

Image:Westermann 1911 Sudansprachen cover.jpg *Source*: http://en.wikipedia.org/w/index.php?title=File:Westermann_1911_Sudansprachen_cover.jpg *License*: unknown *Contributors*: Calmer Waters, Mark Dingemanse, Sfan00 IMG

Image:Niger-Congo map.png *Source*: http://en.wikipedia.org/w/index.php?title=File:Niger-Congo_map.png *License*: unknown *Contributors*: User:Ulamm

Image:Nigeria Benin Cameroon languages.png *Source*: http://en.wikipedia.org/w/index.php?title=File:Nigeria_Benin_Cameroon_languages.png *License*: unknown *Contributors*: User:Ulamm

Image:Niger-Congo speakers.png *Source*: http://en.wikipedia.org/w/index.php?title=File:Niger-Congo_speakers.png *License*: unknown *Contributors*: User:Ulamm

File:Flag of Guinea-Bissau.svg *Source*: http://en.wikipedia.org/w/index.php?title=File:Flag_of_Guinea-Bissau.svg *License*: unknown *Contributors*: User:SKopp

File:EscudoGuiné-Bissau.png *Source*: http://en.wikipedia.org/w/index.php?title=File:EscudoGuiné-Bissau.png *License*: unknown *Contributors*: User:Domaleixo

File:LocationGuineaBissau.svg *Source*: http://en.wikipedia.org/w/index.php?title=File:LocationGuineaBissau.svg *License*: unknown *Contributors*: User:Vardion

Image:Speakerlink.svg *Source*: http://en.wikipedia.org/w/index.php?title=File:Speakerlink.svg *License*: unknown *Contributors*: Woodstone. Original uploader was Woodstone at en.wikipedia

File:Portugal Colonial War 1970.jpg *Source*: http://en.wikipedia.org/w/index.php?title=File:Portugal_Colonial_War_1970.jpg *License*: unknown *Contributors*: User:Roxanna

File:Guinea bissau sm03.png *Source*: http://en.wikipedia.org/w/index.php?title=File:Guinea_bissau_sm03.png *License*: unknown *Contributors*: Dubaduba, Mathias-S

File:Bissau1.jpg *Source*: http://en.wikipedia.org/w/index.php?title=File:Bissau1.jpg *License*: unknown *Contributors*: Colleen Taugher from Lewiston Idaho, USA

File:GW-region.svg *Source*: http://en.wikipedia.org/w/index.php?title=File:GW-region.svg *License*: unknown *Contributors*: Acntx, DTR

File:Paesaggio Guinea-Bissau0001.JPG *Source*: http://en.wikipedia.org/w/index.php?title=File:Paesaggio_Guinea-Bissau0001.JPG *License*: unknown *Contributors*: User:Francofranco56

File:Satellite image of Guinea-Bissau in January 2003.jpg *Source*: http://en.wikipedia.org/w/index.php?title=File:Satellite_image_of_Guinea-Bissau_in_January_2003.jpg *License*: unknown *Contributors*: Jacques Descloitres, MODIS Rapid Response Team, NASA/GSFC

File:Klimadiagramm-deutsch-Bissau-Guinea-Bissau.png *Source*: http://en.wikipedia.org/w/index.php?title=File:Klimadiagramm-deutsch-Bissau-Guinea-Bissau.png *License*: unknown *Contributors*: Hedwig in Washington

File:Villaggio Guinea-Bissau.JPG *Source*: http://en.wikipedia.org/w/index.php?title=File:Villaggio_Guinea-Bissau.JPG *License*: unknown *Contributors*: User:Francofranco56

File:Guinea-bissau-bissau-1.jpg *Source*: http://en.wikipedia.org/w/index.php?title=File:Guinea-bissau-bissau-1.jpg *License*: unknown *Contributors*: User:Kode12

File:Bissau5.jpg *Source*: http://en.wikipedia.org/w/index.php?title=File:Bissau5.jpg *License*: unknown *Contributors*: Colleen Taugher from Lewiston Idaho, USA

Image:PD-icon.svg *Source*: http://en.wikipedia.org/w/index.php?title=File:PD-icon.svg *License*: unknown *Contributors*: User:Duesentrieb, User:Rfl

File:Flag of Sierra Leone.svg *Source*: http://en.wikipedia.org/w/index.php?title=File:Flag_of_Sierra_Leone.svg *License*: unknown *Contributors*: Anime Addict AA, Fry1989, Klemen Kocjancic, Kookaburra, Mattes, Nightstallion, Rocket000, ThomasPusch, Zscout370, 1 anonymous edits

File:Coat_of_arms_of_Sierra_Leone.svg *Source*: http://en.wikipedia.org/w/index.php?title=File:Coat_of_arms_of_Sierra_Leone.svg *License*: unknown *Contributors*: User:Bluebear2, User:Rinaldum, User:S@m, User:Thommy9, User:Yuma, User:Zigeuner

File:Location Sierra Leone AU Africa.svg *Source*: http://en.wikipedia.org/w/index.php?title=File:Location_Sierra_Leone_AU_Africa.svg *License*: unknown *Contributors*: User:Alvaro1984 18

File:Increase2.svg *Source*: http://en.wikipedia.org/w/index.php?title=File:Increase2.svg *License*: unknown *Contributors*: Sarang

File:Prehistoric pottery shards, Sierra Leone.jpg *Source*: http://en.wikipedia.org/w/index.php?title=File:Prehistoric_pottery_shards,_Sierra_Leone.jpg *License*: unknown *Contributors*: John Atherton

File:slaves sierra leone.jpg *Source*: http://en.wikipedia.org/w/index.php?title=File:Slaves_sierra_leone.jpg *License*: unknown *Contributors*: User:Kitkatcrazy

File:Freetown2.jpg *Source*: http://en.wikipedia.org/w/index.php?title=File:Freetown2.jpg *License*: unknown *Contributors*: User:Kitkatcrazy

File:Bai Bureh.jpg *Source*: http://en.wikipedia.org/w/index.php?title=File:Bai_Bureh.jpg *License*: unknown *Contributors*: Ahanta, Ji-Elle, Wst

File:British Expeditionary Force in Freetown, 1919.jpg *Source*: http://en.wikipedia.org/w/index.php?title=File:British_Expeditionary_Force_in_Freetown,_1919.jpg *License*: unknown *Contributors*: New York Times, Co.

Image:All People's Congress political rally Sierra Leone 1968.jpg *Source*: http://en.wikipedia.org/w/index.php?title=File:All_People's_Congress_political_rally_Sierra_Leone_1968.jpg *License*: unknown *Contributors*: John Atherton

Image:School destroyed by Sierra Leone Civil War.jpg *Source*: http://en.wikipedia.org/w/index.php?title=File:School_destroyed_by_Sierra_Leone_Civil_War.jpg *License*: unknown *Contributors*: Laura Lartigue

Image:Sierra_Leone_sat.png *Source*: http://en.wikipedia.org/w/index.php?title=File:Sierra_Leone_sat.png *License*: unknown *Contributors*: Cwolfsheep, Lokal Profil, Martin H.

File:Ernest Bai Koroma.jpg *Source*: http://en.wikipedia.org/w/index.php?title=File:Ernest_Bai_Koroma.jpg *License*: unknown *Contributors*: Valter Campanato/ABr

File:Freetown Court 1984.jpg *Source*: http://en.wikipedia.org/w/index.php?title=File:Freetown_Court_1984.jpg *License*: unknown *Contributors*: Brian Harrington Spier

File:Embassy of Sierra Leone.JPG *Source*: http://en.wikipedia.org/w/index.php?title=File:Embassy_of_Sierra_Leone.JPG *License*: unknown *Contributors*: User:AgnosticPreachersKid

File:Sierra Leone Districts.png *Source*: http://en.wikipedia.org/w/index.php?title=File:Sierra_Leone_Districts.png *License*: unknown *Contributors*: Aliman5040, Martin H.

File:Diamond miners-1-.jpg *Source*: http://en.wikipedia.org/w/index.php?title=File:Diamond_miners-1-.jpg *License*: unknown *Contributors*: Laura Lartigue.

File:Sierra Leone village woman.jpg *Source*: http://en.wikipedia.org/w/index.php?title=File:Sierra_Leone_village_woman.jpg *License*: unknown *Contributors*: LindsayStark

Image:Classroom at a seconday school in Pendembu Sierra Leone.jpg *Source*: http://en.wikipedia.org/w/index.php?title=File:Classroom_at_a_seconday_school_in_Pendembu_Sierra_Leone.jpg *License*: unknown *Contributors*: L. Lartigue

File:Second grade class in Koidu Sierra Leone.jpg *Source*: http://en.wikipedia.org/w/index.php?title=File:Second_grade_class_in_Koidu_Sierra_Leone.jpg *License*: unknown *Contributors*: L. Lartigue

File:Kailahun Government Hospital.jpg *Source*: http://en.wikipedia.org/w/index.php?title=File:Kailahun_Government_Hospital.jpg *License*: unknown *Contributors*: Laura Lartigue

File:Kenema-Kailahun Road.jpg *Source*: http://en.wikipedia.org/w/index.php?title=File:Kenema-Kailahun_Road.jpg *License*: unknown *Contributors*: Lindsay Stark

File:SheriffSumawiki1.jpg *Source*: http://en.wikipedia.org/w/index.php?title=File:SheriffSumawiki1.jpg *License*: unknown *Contributors*: User:LemarvelLemarve

File:Radio listener in Sierra Leone.jpg *Source*: http://en.wikipedia.org/w/index.php?title=File:Radio_listener_in_Sierra_Leone.jpg *License*: unknown *Contributors*: Laura Lartigue

File:Isata Mahoi radio editor and actress.jpg *Source*: http://en.wikipedia.org/w/index.php?title=File:Isata_Mahoi_radio_editor_and_actress.jpg *License*: unknown *Contributors*: Laura Lartigue

File:Flag of Guinea.svg *Source*: http://en.wikipedia.org/w/index.php?title=File:Flag_of_Guinea.svg *License*: unknown *Contributors*: User:SKopp

File:Guinea crest01.png *Source*: http://en.wikipedia.org/w/index.php?title=File:Guinea_crest01.png *License*: unknown *Contributors*: Ttzavaras

File:Guinea (orthographic projection).svg *Source*: http://en.wikipedia.org/w/index.php?title=File:Guinea_(orthographic_projection).svg *License*: unknown *Contributors*: User:Marcos Elias de Oliveira Júnior

File:22novemberdetail.JPG *Source*: http://en.wikipedia.org/w/index.php?title=File:22novemberdetail.JPG *License*: unknown *Contributors*: User:Soman

File:Guinea Regions.png *Source*: http://en.wikipedia.org/w/index.php?title=File:Guinea_Regions.png *License*: unknown *Contributors*: User:Acntx

Image:Guinea_sat.png *Source*: http://en.wikipedia.org/w/index.php?title=File:Guinea_sat.png *License*: unknown *Contributors*: Cwolfsheep, Lokal Profil, Martin H.

File:GuineaMap.png *Source*: http://en.wikipedia.org/w/index.php?title=File:GuineaMap.png *License*: unknown *Contributors*: CIA

File:Guinee Fouta Djalon Doucky.jpg *Source*: http://en.wikipedia.org/w/index.php?title=File:Guinee_Fouta_Djalon_Doucky.jpg *License*: unknown *Contributors*: Haypo

File:Conakrymosque.jpg *Source*: http://en.wikipedia.org/w/index.php?title=File:Conakrymosque.jpg *License*: unknown *Contributors*: MJM Keating

Image:Guinea schoolgirls.jpg *Source*: http://en.wikipedia.org/w/index.php?title=File:Guinea_schoolgirls.jpg *License*: unknown *Contributors*: Laura Lartigue (USAID)

GNU Free Documentation License Version 1.2, November 2002 Copyright (C) 2000,2001,2002 Free Software Foundation, Inc. 59 Temple Place, Suite 330, Boston, MA 02111-1307 USA Everyone is permitted to copy and distribute verbatim copies of this license document, but changing it is not allowed.

0. PREAMBLE

The purpose of this License is to make a manual, textbook, or other functional and useful document "free" in the sense of freedom: to assure everyone the effective freedom to copy and redistribute it, with or without modifying it, either commercially or noncommercially. Secondarily, this License preserves for the author and publisher a way to get credit for their work, while not being considered responsible for modifications made by others. This License is a kind of "copyleft", which means that derivative works of the document must themselves be free in the same sense. It complements the GNU General Public License, which is a copyleft license designed for free software. We have designed this License in order to use it for manuals for free software, because free software needs free documentation: a free program should come with manuals providing the same freedoms that the software does. But this License is not limited to software manuals; it can be used for any textual work, regardless of subject matter or whether it is published as a printed book. We recommend this License principally for works whose purpose is instruction or reference.

1. APPLICABILITY AND DEFINITIONS

This License applies to any manual or other work, in any medium, that contains a notice placed by the copyright holder saying it can be distributed under the terms of this License. Such a notice grants a world-wide, royalty-free license, unlimited in duration, to use that work under the conditions stated herein. The "Document", below, refers to any such manual or work. Any member of the public is a licensee, and is addressed as "you". You accept the license if you copy, modify or distribute the work in a way requiring permission under copyright law. A "Modified Version" of the Document means any work containing the Document or a portion of it, either copied verbatim, or with modifications and/or translated into another language. A "Secondary Section" is a named appendix or a front-matter section of the Document that deals exclusively with the relationship of the publishers or authors of the Document to the Document's overall subject (or to related matters) and contains nothing that could fall directly within that overall subject. (Thus, if the Document is in part a textbook of mathematics, a Secondary Section may not explain any mathematics.) The relationship could be a matter of historical connection with the subject or with related matters, or of legal, commercial, philosophical, ethical or political position regarding them. The "Invariant Sections" are certain Secondary Sections whose titles are designated, as being those of Invariant Sections, in the notice that says that the Document is released under this License. If a section does not fit the above definition of Secondary then it is not allowed to be designated as Invariant. The Document may contain zero Invariant Sections. If the Document does not identify any Invariant Sections then there are none. The "Cover Texts" are certain short passages of text that are listed, as Front-Cover Texts or Back-Cover Texts, in the notice that says that the Document is released under this License. A Front-Cover Text may be at most 5 words, and a Back-Cover Text may be at most 25 words. A "Transparent" copy of the Document means a machine-readable copy, represented in a format whose specification is available to the general public, that is suitable for revising the document straightforwardly with generic text editors or (for images composed of pixels) generic paint programs or (for drawings) some widely available drawing editor, and that is suitable for input to text formatters or for automatic translation to a variety of formats suitable for input to text formatters. A copy made in an otherwise Transparent file format whose markup, or absence of markup, has been arranged to thwart or discourage subsequent modification by readers is not Transparent. An image format is not Transparent if used for any substantial amount of text. A copy that is not "Transparent" is called "Opaque". Examples of suitable formats for Transparent copies include plain ASCII without markup, Texinfo input format, LaTeX input format, SGML or XML using a publicly available DTD, and standard-conforming simple HTML, PostScript or PDF designed for human modification. Examples of transparent image formats include PNG, XCF and JPG. Opaque formats include proprietary formats that can be read and edited only by proprietary word processors, SGML or XML for which the DTD and/or processing tools are not generally available, and the machine-generated HTML, PostScript or PDF produced by some word processors for output purposes only. The "Title Page" means, for a printed book, the title page itself, plus such following pages as are needed to hold, legibly, the material this License requires to appear in the title page. For works in formats which do not have any title page as such, "Title Page" means the text near the most prominent appearance of the work's title, preceding the beginning of the body of the text. A section "Entitled XYZ" means a named subunit of the Document whose title either is precisely XYZ or contains XYZ in parentheses following text that translates XYZ in another language. (Here XYZ stands for a specific section name mentioned below, such as "Acknowledgements", "Dedications", "Endorsements", or "History".) To "Preserve the Title" of such a section when you modify the Document means that it remains a section "Entitled XYZ" according to this definition. The Document may include Warranty Disclaimers next to the notice which states that this License applies to the Document. These Warranty Disclaimers are considered to be included by reference in this License, but only as regards disclaiming warranties: any other implication that these Warranty Disclaimers may have is void and has no effect on the meaning of this License.

2. VERBATIM COPYING

You may copy and distribute the Document in any medium, either commercially or noncommercially, provided that this License, the copyright notices, and the license notice saying this License applies to the Document are reproduced in all copies, and that you add no other conditions whatsoever to those of this License. You may not use technical measures to obstruct or control the reading or further copying of the copies you make or distribute. However, you may accept compensation in exchange for copies. If you distribute a large enough number of copies you must also follow the conditions in section 3. You may also lend copies, under the same conditions stated above, and you may publicly display copies.

3. COPYING IN QUANTITY

If you publish printed copies (or copies in media that commonly have printed covers) of the Document, numbering more than 100, and the Document's license notice requires Cover Texts, you must enclose the copies in covers that carry, clearly and legibly, all these Cover Texts: Front-Cover Texts on the front cover, and Back-Cover Texts on the back cover. Both covers must also clearly and legibly identify you as the publisher of these copies. The front cover must present the full title with all words of the title equally prominent and visible. You may add other material on the covers in addition. Copying with changes limited to the covers, as long as they preserve the title of the Document and satisfy these conditions, can be treated as verbatim copying in other respects. If the required texts for either cover are too voluminous to fit legibly, you should put the first ones listed (as many as fit reasonably) on the actual cover, and continue the rest onto adjacent pages. If you publish or distribute Opaque copies of the Document numbering more than 100, you must either include a machine-readable Transparent copy along with each Opaque copy, or state in or with each Opaque copy a computer-network location from which the general network-using public has access to download using public-standard network protocols a complete Transparent copy of the Document, free of added material. If you use the latter option, you must take reasonably prudent steps, when you begin distribution of Opaque copies in quantity, to ensure that this Transparent copy will remain thus accessible at the stated location until at least one year after the last time you distribute an Opaque copy (directly or through your agents or retailers) of that edition to the public. It is requested, but not required, that you contact the authors of the Document well before redistributing any large number of copies, to give them a chance to provide you with an updated version of the Document.

4. MODIFICATIONS

You may copy and distribute a Modified Version of the Document under the conditions of sections 2 and 3 above, provided that you release the Modified Version under precisely this License, with the Modified Version filling the role of the Document, thus licensing distribution and modification of the Modified Version to whoever possesses a copy of it. In addition, you must do these things in the Modified Version: A. Use in the Title Page (and on the covers, if any) a title distinct from that of the Document, and from those of previous versions (which should, if there were any, be listed in the History section of the Document). You may use the same title as a previous version if the original publisher of that version gives permission. B. List on the Title Page, as authors, one or more persons or entities responsible for authorship of the modifications in the Modified Version, together with at least five of the principal authors of the Document (all of its principal authors, if it has fewer than five), unless they release you from this requirement. C. State on the Title page the name of the publisher of the Modified Version, as the publisher. D. Preserve all the copyright notices of the Document. E. Add an appropriate copyright notice for your modifications adjacent to the other copyright notices. F. Include, immediately after the copyright notices, a license notice giving the public permission to use the Modified Version under the terms of this License, in the form shown in the Addendum below. G. Preserve in that license notice the full lists of Invariant Sections and required Cover Texts given in the Document's license notice. H. Include an unaltered copy of this License. I. Preserve the section Entitled "History", Preserve its Title, and add to it an item stating at least the title, year, new authors, and publisher of the Modified Version as given on the Title Page. If there is no section Entitled "History" in the Document, create one stating the title, year, authors, and publisher of the Document as given on its Title Page, then add an item describing the Modified Version as stated in the previous sentence. J. Preserve the network location, if any, given in the Document for public access to a Transparent copy of the Document, and likewise the network locations given in the Document for previous versions it was based on. These may be placed in the "History" section. You may omit a network location for a work that was published at least four years before the Document itself, or if the original publisher of the version it refers to gives permission. K. For any section Entitled "Acknowledgements" or "Dedications", Preserve the Title of the section, and preserve in the section all the substance and tone of each of the contributor acknowledgements and/or dedications given therein. L. Preserve all the Invariant Sections of the Document, unaltered in their text and in their titles. Section numbers or the equivalent are not considered part of the section titles. M. Delete any section Entitled "Endorsements". Such a section may not be included in the Modified Version. N. Do not retitle any existing section to be Entitled "Endorsements" or to conflict in title with any Invariant Section. O. Preserve any Warranty Disclaimers. If the Modified Version includes new front-matter sections or appendices that qualify as Secondary Sections and contain no material copied from the Document, you may at your option designate some or all of these sections as invariant. To do this, add their titles to the list of Invariant Sections in the Modified Version's license notice. These titles must be distinct from any other section titles. You may add a section Entitled "Endorsements", provided it contains nothing but endorsements of your Modified Version by various parties--for example, statements of peer review or that the text has been approved by an organization as the authoritative definition of a standard. You may add a passage of up to five words as a Front-Cover Text, and a passage of up to 25 words as a Back-Cover Text, to the end of the list of Cover Texts in the Modified Version. Only one passage of Front-Cover Text and one of Back-Cover Text may be added by (or through arrangements made by) any one entity. If the Document already includes a cover text for the same cover, previously added by you or by arrangement made by the same entity you are acting on behalf of, you may not add another; but you may replace the old one, on explicit permission from the previous publisher that added the old one. The author(s) and publisher(s) of the Document do not by this License give permission to use their names for publicity for or to assert or imply endorsement of any Modified Version.

5. COMBINING DOCUMENTS

You may combine the Document with other documents released under this License, under the terms defined in section 4 above for modified versions, provided that you include in the combination all of the Invariant Sections of all of the original documents, unmodified, and list them all as Invariant Sections of your combined work in its license notice, and that you preserve all their Warranty Disclaimers. The combined work need only contain one copy of this License, and multiple identical Invariant Sections may be replaced with a single copy. If there are multiple Invariant Sections with the same name but different contents, make the title of each such section unique by adding at the end of it, in parentheses, the name of the original author or publisher of that section if known, or else a unique number. Make the same adjustment to the section titles in the list of Invariant Sections in the license notice of the combined work. In the combination, you must combine any sections Entitled "History" in the various original documents, forming one section Entitled "History"; likewise combine any sections Entitled "Acknowledgements", and any sections Entitled "Dedications". You must delete all sections Entitled "Endorsements".

6. COLLECTIONS OF DOCUMENTS

You may make a collection consisting of the Document and other documents released under this License, and replace the individual copies of this License in the various documents with a single copy that is included in the collection, provided that you follow the rules of this License for verbatim copying of each of the documents in all other respects. You may extract a single document from such a collection, and distribute it individually under this License, provided you insert a copy of this License into the extracted document, and follow this License in all other respects regarding verbatim copying of that document.

7. AGGREGATION WITH INDEPENDENT WORKS

A compilation of the Document or its derivatives with other separate and independent documents or works, in or on a volume of a storage or distribution medium, is called an "aggregate" if the copyright resulting from the compilation is not used to limit the legal rights of the compilation's users beyond what the individual works permit. When the Document is included in an aggregate, this License does not apply to the other works in the aggregate which are not themselves derivative works of the Document. If the Cover Text requirement of section 3 is applicable to these copies of the Document, then if the Document is less than one half of the entire aggregate, the Document's Cover Texts may be placed on covers that bracket the Document within the aggregate, or the electronic equivalent of covers if the Document is in electronic form. Otherwise they must appear on printed covers that bracket the whole aggregate.

8. TRANSLATION

Translation is considered a kind of modification, so you may distribute translations of the Document under the terms of section 4. Replacing Invariant Sections with translations requires special permission from their copyright holders, but you may include translations of some or all Invariant Sections in addition to the original versions of these Invariant Sections. You may include a translation of this License, and all the license notices in the Document, and any Warranty Disclaimers, provided that you also include the original English version of this License and the original versions of those notices and disclaimers. In case of a disagreement between the translation and the original version of this License or a notice or disclaimer, the original version will prevail. If a section in the Document is Entitled "Acknowledgements", "Dedications", or "History", the requirement (section 4) to Preserve its Title (section 1) will typically require changing the actual title.

9. TERMINATION

You may not copy, modify, sublicense, or distribute the Document except as expressly provided for under this License. Any other attempt to copy, modify, sublicense or distribute the Document is void, and will automatically terminate your rights under this License. However, parties who have received copies, or rights, from you under this License will not have their licenses terminated so long as such parties remain in full compliance.

10. FUTURE REVISIONS OF THIS LICENSE

The Free Software Foundation may publish new, revised versions of the GNU Free Documentation License from time to time. Such new versions will be similar in spirit to the present version, but may differ in detail to address new problems or concerns. See http://www.gnu.org/copyleft/. Each version of the License is given a distinguishing version number. If the Document specifies that a particular numbered version of this License "or any later version" applies to it, you have the option of following the terms and conditions either of that specified version or of any later version that has been published (not as a draft) by the Free Software Foundation. If the Document does not specify a version number of this License, you may choose any version ever published (not as a draft) by the Free Software Foundation. ADDENDUM: How to use this License for your documents To use this License in a document you have written, include a copy of the License in the document and put the following copyright and license notices just after the title page: Copyright (c) YEAR YOUR NAME. Permission is granted to copy, distribute and/or modify this document under the terms of the GNU Free Documentation License, Version 1.2 or any later version published by the Free Software Foundation; with no Invariant Sections, no Front-Cover Texts, and no Back-Cover Texts. A copy of the license is included in the section entitled "GNU Free Documentation License". If you have Invariant Sections, Front-Cover Texts and Back-Cover Texts, replace the "with...Texts." line with this: with the Invariant Sections being LIST THEIR TITLES, with the Front-Cover Texts being LIST, and with the Back-Cover Texts being LIST. If you have Invariant Sections without Cover Texts, or some other combination of the three, merge those two alternatives to suit the situation. If your document contains nontrivial examples of program code, we recommend releasing these examples in parallel under your choice of free software license, such as the GNU General Public License, to permit their use in free software.

CPSIA information can be obtained at www.ICGtesting.com
Printed in the USA
LVOW051011160712

290236LV00002B/89/P